INTRODUCTION

Megawords introduces procedures for teaching the reading and spelling of multisyllabic words through a multisensory approach. The program is the result of our experience teaching learning disabled children and adults. However, the techniques described will be useful to teachers of any population for which the goal is word attack skills for words with more than one syllable.

In working with learning disabled students, adults, and others with reading and spelling difficulties, we noted a lack of appropriate materials for teaching the reading and spelling of multisyllabic words. Numerous programs exist for instruction of phonic generalizations found in one-syllable words. While many materials include phonic elements of multisyllabic word patterns, few provide a format to assess skills, pinpoint weaknesses, teach required subskills, and monitor progress systematically. The dearth of materials for teaching skills in this area is a major problem for teachers whose students have reached a fourth- or fifth-grade reading and/or spelling level. Many students have difficulty advancing beyond this level, at which mastery of multisyllabic words becomes necessary. Our need to create a program to teach the more advanced reading and spelling skills became paramount.

At first it seemed impossible to design a structured format for teaching multisyllabic words because of their phonic complexity. As we developed the program, however, it became clear that the English language could be analyzed into components that demonstrate an amazing degree of regularity and consistency. We developed controlled word lists that build sequentially on phonic and structural elements. Some words are appropriately placed on more than one list. Some lists include words with phonic elements that are not focused on until later in the sequence. Though the lists are not perfectly inclusive or exclusive, each emphasizes a significant and recurring phonic element of the English language. Students can be encouraged to add new words to lists as they study them.

GENERAL DESCRIPTION OF *MEGAWORDS*

Megawords combines several principles found to be effective in teaching students with language learning difficulties. These principles, combined and specifically applied to the teaching of multisyllabic words, make *Megawords* unique.

- *Megawords* teaches phonic regularities. The lists are structured according to phonic elements. This approach stresses the teaching of rules and generalizations as a tool for sounding out and spelling unfamiliar words. The words are not to be taught as sight words unless indicated.

- *Megawords* is multisensory. Specific teaching instructions are provided to ensure that students use their auditory, visual, and kinesthetic modalities when learning a skill. The process of seeing, saying, hearing, and writing is a major key to success. Thus, the students practice spelling the words as they learn to read them.

- *Megawords* is systematic. There is no guesswork as to what students need to be taught or when to advance them through the program. A skills Check Test assesses each student's skills by pinpointing deficits and identifying specific instructional goals. Systematic monitoring of progress by use of the Accuracy Checklist for recording accuracy and of the Proficiency Graph for recording reading rate is an integral part of the program.

- *Megawords* is task analytic. The words on each list are analyzed and broken down into their component subskills and presented in sequential learning steps. Though the final objective is for students to read and spell the words with automaticity, they often need specific instruction on the intervening steps. When they use this method, their success is guaranteed.

- *Megawords* is adaptable to the individual's needs. The task analytic nature of the program makes this possible. Some students may master a word list with minimal drill on the sequential learning steps. Others will require more instructional time on each step. Goals for accuracy and proficiency are determined on an individual basis.

- *Megawords* is adaptable to the teacher's needs. It may be used for classroom instruction or for one-to-one tutoring. In a classroom setting, students can chart and graph their own progress. They can also learn to time each other for proficiency and to test each other for accuracy. The charts and graphs allow easy monitoring of the progress recorded by the students. The word lists can serve as a supplement to the regular reading program and the sequence can be adapted to correspond to other materials.

- *Megawords* encourages student involvement. Most students are motivated to progress when goals are identified for them. The structured format of this program specifies what is to be learned and how well it is to be learned. Because students can monitor their own progress, they can move at their own pace rather than that of the class average. Group or individual rewards for mastering skills can be used to motivate students.

- *Megawords* may be used by paraprofessionals. Teacher's aides, volunteers, and peer tutors can easily follow the instructions. Explanations for administration of the Check Test, teaching concepts, and monitoring progress are written in clear and simple language. With minimal effort, teachers can supervise and train paraprofessionals to use *Megawords* so that instruction can be individualized.

OVERVIEW OF TEACHING STRATEGIES

Megawords teaches the reading, spelling, and contextual use of multisyllabic words through a systematic progression of skills. Each book focuses on a distinct group of phonic skills; teaching strategies throughout the program are uniform.

For multisensory teaching to be successful, students need to practice spelling words while they learn to read them. This procedure provides the necessary simultaneous input through all the processing channels (visual, auditory, and kinesthetic). However, the approach used to teach spelling to low-skilled students differs in emphasis from that used to teach them reading. For reading, the goal is to teach students word attack skills that they can apply to decoding (sounding out) unfamiliar words. Thus, it is desirable to present to the students a large number of words that they may never have seen before in order to challenge their understanding of the concepts taught.

In contrast, the number of words required for spelling mastery should be limited for low-skilled students because spelling is a much more complex skill. Multisyllabic words frequently contain the schwa sound, which can be spelled with any of the five vowels. While this does not typically present a reading problem for students, it is a major barrier for those students who must learn to spell phonetically. This difficulty also applies to other vowel and consonant sounds that can be spelled in more than one way. The spelling task is usually further complicated by students' not receiving immediate feedback on their performances. For these reasons it is not feasible for severely learning disabled or low-skilled students to learn the correct spelling of all the words on the lists. Rather, students should learn to spell a limited number of useful words *well*. On each list we identify with an asterisk *practical spelling words* that the students are likely to use in writing. Teachers and students should feel free to add to or delete these words to suit their needs.

The procedures for using the *Megawords* materials are outlined below. You should familiarize yourself with these teaching strategies before using the program.

ASSESSMENT OF READING AND SPELLING SKILLS

Each book contains a detailed Check Test, which will specifically pinpoint skill deficits and, thus, identify which lists should be the focal point of instruction. This Check Test should be given as a pretest before students start a book. It can be readministered after students complete the book if posttest scores are desired. The Book 2 Check Test and instructions for administration are found on pages 10-11.

LEARNING STEPS

A discussion of relevant rules and concepts introduces each list. Six sequential learning steps follow; they lead to the final objective — reading and spelling words with automaticity. This task breakdown analyzes words according to their phonetic elements and then presents them in a parts-to-whole fashion.

Worksheets for each learning step enable students to acquire the necessary skills gradually. In this way, they experience greater success. Some students may proceed through all the steps rapidly or may even bypass some steps. Others may require prolonged drill and supplemental activities. Pacing will depend on the individual student's needs.

The Task Breakdown for Teaching the Coding of Multisyllabic Words on page 4 summarizes the six learning steps that are the backbone of *Megawords*. Each step includes both a decoding (reading) and an encoding (spelling) task. The left half of the chart indicates the decoding subskills; the right half, the encoding subskills. The tasks required at each step are as follows:

STEP 1. Work with the Isolated Word Parts

Drill on the isolated word parts is a necessary first step. This may entail identifying types of syllables or working on prefixes, suffixes, or special vowel and consonant combinations. Worksheets require the students both to read and spell the word parts. In addition, we recommend that students get additional practice on the isolated parts by using drill cards. Instructions for using drill cards in teaching specific skills are provided in each book.

STEP 2. Work with the Combined Word Parts

For this step, students are required to recognize word parts within words, combine them, and read a whole word. The reverse procedure is required for spelling: the teacher dictates a whole word and the students must isolate and spell the word parts. At first, students should say the isolated word parts aloud before spelling them. Eventually, they can say them to themselves. Practice with common spelling patterns for the schwa sound is included when relevant. This step is crucial and should not be bypassed.

Students are sometimes asked to mark vowels in words with an unaccented syllable. Some dictionaries list both the schwa and the short-*i* sounds as acceptable pronunciations and some vary on the choice. Regional accents also affect the pronunciation of these words. For these reasons, do not insist that students always know the technically correct vowel sound as long as they can decode the word.

In Step 2 — Reading, words are presented as detached syllables as an intermediate step to help students identify the correct vowel sound before having to tackle whole words. You may notice that syllabication in *Megawords* is closer to that used for hyphenation than that found in pronunciation guides in a dictionary (*chat-ter* rather than /chat·er/, *dis-cus-sion* rather than /dis·kəsh·ən/). Syllabication is presented as simply as possible to avoid confusing the students with technical syllabication rules.

STEP 3. Work with the Whole Word

If students have had sufficient drill on Steps 1 and 2, reading and spelling the whole word should be relatively easy. For reading, they practice applying relevant word attack skills. Worksheets require them to divide whole words into syllables and to pronounce them. The spelling worksheets for Step 3 focus on words frequently used in writing. Students practice spelling the recurring phonic elements in common words. Spelling rules and generalizations are also presented in Step 3. Proofreading, the detection and correction of spelling errors, is a necessary and important skill for all students. Step 3 exercises provide practice in this skill.

TASK BREAKDOWN FOR TEACHING THE CODING
OF MULTISYLLABIC WORDS

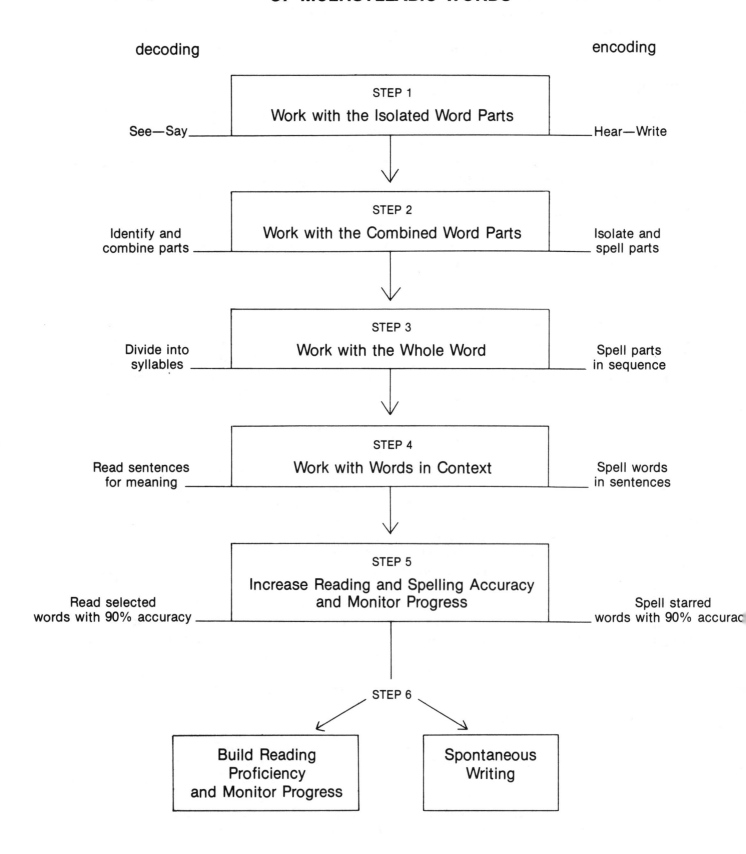

decoding   encoding

STEP 1
Work with the Isolated Word Parts

See—Say   Hear—Write

STEP 2
Work with the Combined Word Parts

Identify and   Isolate and
combine parts   spell parts

STEP 3
Work with the Whole Word

Divide into   Spell parts
syllables   in sequence

STEP 4
Work with Words in Context

Read sentences   Spell words
for meaning   in sentences

STEP 5
Increase Reading and Spelling Accuracy
and Monitor Progress

Read selected   Spell starred
words with 90% accuracy   words with 90% accurac

STEP 6

Build Reading
Proficiency
and Monitor Progress

Spontaneous
Writing

STEP 4. Work with Words in Context

This step provides an opportunity for students to apply their coding skills by using the words in context. Worksheets on vocabulary encourage them to learn word meanings from context as well as to develop dictionary skills. Reading and spelling sentences that emphasize the specific phonic element in each list are also part of this step.

STEP 5. Increase Reading and Spelling Accuracy and Monitor Progress

Students who have successfully completed Steps 1 through 4 are ready for a skill check on reading and spelling. Randomly select ten words from the list for the reading skill check. Ten starred words from the list can be dictated to test spelling accuracy. Skill checks should be repeated until students have achieved 90 percent accuracy or better.

The columns of many of the lists are organized according to vowel sound, prefix, or suffix. Some students may find it less frustrating to read *down* the columns initially, focusing on one pattern at a time. Subsequently, they can read the list by rows, alternating the word patterns.

Have your students record their progress in reading and spelling accuracy on the Accuracy Checklists. A copy of the Accuracy Checklist is provided on page 68 and in the student's workbook. Reading and spelling accuracy scores should be recorded to the right of the Check Test Scores column. These scores can be written as fractions: number correct over number attempted. The date when an accuracy check is done should be noted as well. When students have achieved 90 percent accuracy, they can shade in the box to indicate mastery. The sample Accuracy Checklist below demonstrates its use for record keeping.

The Accuracy Checklist is essential for monitoring your students' progress. It not only enables you to make appropriate instructional decisions but also provides valuable feedback to your students that they are, indeed, improving their skills.

ACCURACY CHECKLIST

Student _Sue Smith_

Record accuracy score as a fraction: $\dfrac{\text{\# correct}}{\text{\# attempted}}$

List	Examples	Check Test Scores Date: 10/10		Reading			Spelling		
		Reading	Spelling	10/10			10/12	10/14	10/17
9. Consonant Suffixes and Plurals -ly, -ty, -ful, -fully, -ment, -less, -ness, -some, -s, -es	careless statement branches	$\dfrac{5}{5}$	$\dfrac{3}{5}$	Mastered			$\dfrac{6}{10}$	$\dfrac{8}{10}$	$\dfrac{9}{10}$
				10/12	10/14	10/17	10/19	10/21	
10. Vowel Suffixes and Spelling Rules -ing, -er, -est, -en, -ish, -y	biggest stranger planting	$\dfrac{3}{5}$	$\dfrac{3}{5}$	$\dfrac{6}{10}$	$\dfrac{8}{10}$	$\dfrac{10}{10}$	$\dfrac{7}{10}$	$\dfrac{8}{10}$	
				10/19	10/21				
11. Three Sounds of -ed /d/, /t/, /əd/	tacked mailed painted	$\dfrac{3}{5}$	$\dfrac{1}{5}$	$\dfrac{7}{10}$	$\dfrac{9}{10}$				

STEP 6. Build Reading Proficiency, Monitor Progress, and Encourage Spontaneous Writing

Research indicates that automaticity of decoding skills facilitates reading comprehension and is often a prerequisite to the more complex comprehension skills of reasoning and inference.[1] Students' skills must be automatic (proficient) before they can comprehend a passage or progress to more difficult skills. Thus, once students have demonstrated that they can read the word lists untimed with 90 percent accuracy, they should work on increasing their reading speed by doing frequent rate timings. In our experience, repeated practice and drill are more effective than direct instruction for building proficiency.

Use a stopwatch or second hand to time students as they read the list for a minute. A warm-up timing can be used for practice before doing a second, official, timing. If students finish the list in less than a minute, they should return to the beginning and continue to read until the time is up. Progress is then recorded on the Proficiency Graph, indicating the number of words read correctly in a minute as well as the number of errors. A goal of forty-five to fifty words per minute with two or fewer errors on two of three consecutive days is realistic for most students. This goal can certainly be adjusted for individuals. A sample Proficiency Graph is on page 7. A blank Proficiency Graph is on page 69 and at the back of the student's workbook.

Giving students sufficient practice in spelling words helps the spelling process become automatic. They are then able to concentrate on the content of what they want to express in writing. Their ultimate goal is being able to use correctly spelled words to convey their ideas. Although worksheets on written expression are not included in this program, you should encourage your students to spell the newly learned words in their written work. Creative writing assignments in which students try to include as many words as possible from a given list will provide such an opportunity.

ANALYSIS OF STUDENT PROGRESS FOR DECISION MAKING

Once students have attained 90 percent accuracy in reading words and are working to increase their reading proficiency, instruction should begin on the concepts of the next word list. This way, they will be learning new skills as they improve others. Typically, reading accuracy will be achieved prior to spelling accuracy. Thus, an individual might be working on spelling with List 9, on reading proficiency with List 10, and on reading accuracy with List 11. When you introduce new concepts, include the spelling tasks even if the students are still working to achieve spelling mastery on earlier lists.

If students are not achieving accuracy or proficiency goals, a teaching intervention is necessary. If a student's reading and/or spelling accuracy is not improving, more drill should be done on the learning steps. You can make up games and other creative activities to work on the necessary concepts. Error analysis can help pinpoint the areas of concern. For example, review of a student's mistakes in spelling might reveal difficulty in spelling a specific schwa ending pattern such as -al or -on. You can then provide the necessary drill to remedy the problem.

Lack of progress in reading proficiency also demands attention. If students are making more than four errors on timed readings, discontinue timing them and focus your instruction instead on reading accuracy. Identify and analyze the errors and concentrate your teaching on the specific problem areas. If errors are minimal but the students are not meeting projected goals, they probably need more practice with the words. Marked improvement can often be made if the students practice the word lists at home. Offering rewards, such as special classroom privileges, for attaining goals is also an effective technique. In some cases, it may be appropriate to lower proficiency goals for students who are having difficulty.

[1]E. Haughton, "Aims — Growing and Sharing," in Jordan et al., *Let's Try Doing Something Else Kind of Thing*, Arlington, Va.: The Council for Exceptional Children, 1972.

Barbara Bateman (ed.), *Learning Disorders*, Vol. IV, Seattle, Wash.: Special Child Publications, Inc., 1971.

S.J. Samuels and Patricia Dahl, *A Mastery Based Experimental Program for Teaching Poor Readers High Speed Word Recognition Skills* (Research Report #55), University of Minnesota, 1973.

C. Starlin, "Peers and Precision," *Teaching Exceptional Children*, Vol. 3, No. 3, pp. 129-140, 1971.

PROFICIENCY GRAPH

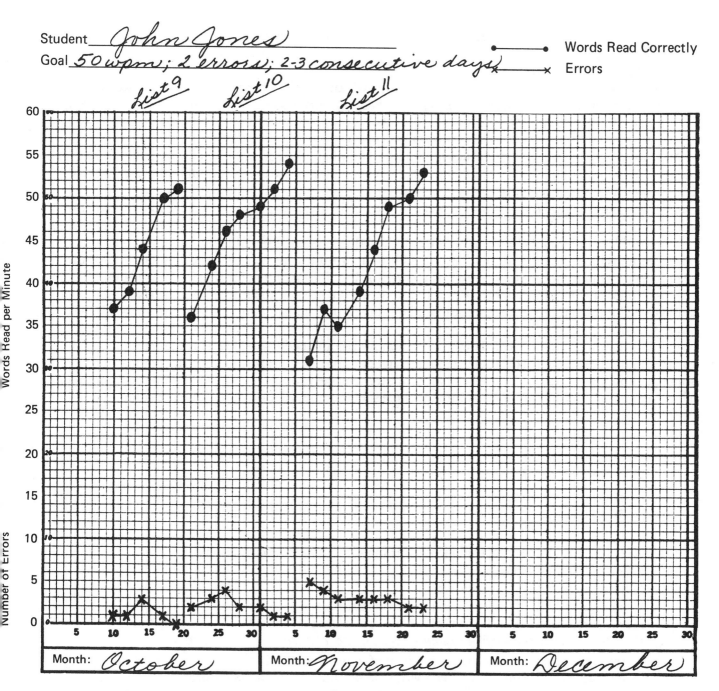

Student _John Jones_

Goal _50 wpm; 2 errors; 2-3 consecutive days_

●——● Words Read Correctly
x——x Errors

List 9   List 10   List 11

Words Read per Minute

Number of Errors

Month: _October_   Month: _November_   Month: _December_

Calendar Days

STUDENT INVOLVEMENT

Student involvement is a *must* throughout all of the learning steps just discussed. Students should be aware of their Check Test results, what they know, and what they need to learn. They should be aware of their progress in both reading and spelling accuracy and proficiency. They should know that the learning steps are divided into small parts to help them reach the ultimate goal of reading and writing fluently. We suggest that the teacher either read To the Student at the beginning of the student's workbook with the students or paraphrase and discuss it.

SPECIAL CONSIDERATIONS FOR *MEGAWORDS 2*

Megawords teaches the reading and spelling of multisyllabic words through a systematic progression of skills. Book 1 approaches word attack through syllabication. Book 2 attends to a second coding skill — recognizing prefixes and suffixes.

Megawords 2 (Lists 9–14) focuses on common prefixes and suffixes found in two-syllable words.[1] It emphasizes the spelling rules and generalizations for adding suffixes and the meaning of prefixes. Some instruction on Latin roots is also included so that the students practice meaningful word building. Refer to the summary of prefixes and roots on pages 9 and 10.

Megawords 2 also discusses guidelines for determining where the accent falls in two-syllable words. The accented first syllable, the most common pattern in two-syllable words, was introduced in *Megawords 1*. Lists 13 and 14 instruct students on the alternative accent pattern — the accented second syllable. This pattern becomes the rule for words with prefixes. Generally, the root in the second syllable receives the accent.

The word lists in Book 2 are not exhaustive; rather, they contain a sampling of the more common words with prefixes and suffixes. Feel free to add to the word lists as desired. Teaching the *concept* of reading and spelling words with affixes is the key to instruction. At no point should the students be required to learn words by memory. The goal is to teach the rules of the English language so that students will be able to make generalizations about other, unfamiliar, words and to read and spell them successfully.

For Step 1, working with the isolated word parts, we recommend that students make their own drill cards with prefixes and suffixes. Index cards are suitable for this purpose. For practice with suffixes, students should write the suffix on the front of a card and the pronunciation and key words on the back. They can add key words that demonstrate the three spelling rules when List 10 is introduced.

front   back

Students can test each other on reading and spelling the suffixes, asking questions such as:
1. What are the three sounds of *-ed*?
2. Is *-ed* a vowel or consonant suffix?
3. What is an example of a word having an *-ed* suffix?
4. How do you spell the suffix that places a word in the past tense?
5. How do you spell the suffix in *jumped, called,* and *planted*?

For drill on prefixes, students should write the prefix and the meaning on the front of the card, as illustrated. On the back of the card, they should write the pronunciation and key words.

front   back

[1] Words of greater length will be dealt with in Book 8, which will introduce assimilated prefixes.

Students can work individually or in pairs daily until they can read and spell the prefixes and give the key words. Most students should make recognition, rather than recall, of prefix meanings their goal. A similar procedure may be used to practice roots. Learning to read and spell the isolated roots may be helpful for students; however, we do not recommend that they be required to memorize the meanings of roots. In most cases, the meanings of Latin roots give only a *clue* to word meaning. The low-skilled students will often have difficulty seeing the relationship between the literal meaning (*permit* = "to put through") and the actual meaning of the word. The worksheets on roots and prefixes provide an opportunity to build vocabulary in a meaningful way.

SUMMARY OF PREFIXES

Prefix	Origin*	Meaning	Key Word
re-	L.	back, again	return
de-	L.	down, away from	depress
sub-	L.	below, under	subway
pro-	L.	forward	propel
pre-	L.	before	preschool
per-	L.	through, completely	perspire
un-	A.S.	not	unkind
in-	L.	in, not	intake, insane
ex-	L.	out	exit
a-	A.S.	on, in	aboard
dis-	L.	apart, opposite of	dislike
trans-	L.	across	transmit
mis-	A.S.	wrong, bad	misplace
con-	L.	together, with	connect
ab-	L.	away from	absent
ad-	L.	to, toward	advance
ob-	L.	against, in the way	object
inter-	L.	between, among	interstate

*L. = Latin; A.S. = Anglo-Saxon

SUMMARY OF ROOTS

Root	Origin*	Meaning	Key Word
pel	L.	to drive	propel
tend	L.	to stretch	extend
spire	L.	to breathe	inspire
form	L.	to form	reform
spect	L.	to see, to look	inspect
fect	L.	to make, to do	perfect
scribe	L.	to write	subscribe
port	L.	to carry	export
duct	L.	to lead	conduct
tain	L.	to hold	contain
fer	L.	to carry	transfer
tract	L.	to drag, draw, pull	distract
ject	L.	to throw	reject
mit	L.	to send	transmit
sist	L.	to stand	insist

*L. = Latin

CHECK TEST: LISTS 9–14

ADMINISTERING THE CHECK TEST

The Check Test informally assesses a student's ability to read and spell words that follow the patterns presented in *Megawords 2*. Although the reading test must be administered individually, the spelling test can be administered to a group.

To test reading, give the student the Student's Reading Copy[1] and instruct him or her to read down the columns. Use the Examiner's Recording Form[2] to note errors and mark the number correct. Enough space is provided after each word to write the student's responses so that errors can be analyzed later.

[1] The Student's Reading Copy is on page 71. It may be removed and inserted in a plastic cover.
[2] An Examiner's Recording Form appears on page 70 and at the end of each student's workbook. Remove the student's form for the Check Test and keep it for your files. One side can be used for a pretest and the other, for a posttest.

To test spelling, give the students blank paper and tell them to number from one to five, six times. Dictate the following words to assess their ability to spell frequently used words that follow the patterns presented in Book 2.

9. Consonant Suffixes and Plurals

1. lonely
2. careless
3. churches
4. hopefully
5. copies

10. Vowel Suffixes

1. fastest
2. shining
3. woolen
4. bigger
5. muddy

11. Three Sounds of -ed

1. trimmed
2. asked
3. yelled
4. placed
5. shouted

12. Spelling Patterns—Vowel Suffixes

1. sloppy
2. staring
3. canned
4. scary
5. hoped

13. Common Prefixes

1. reward
2. permit
3. prepare
4. explore
5. subtract

14. Additional Common Prefixes

1. interest
2. dismiss
3. contain
4. awhile
5. transport

Share the test results with your students so that they become aware of the specific word patterns that they need to learn or review. Be sure constantly to reassess the students' skills as you work with them. Often you will discover strengths or weaknesses that were not revealed in the Check Test results.

If a student misses the first two words of a group and it is apparent that the words are too difficult, discontinue testing in that group. Remember that the purpose of the Check Test is simply to identify specific skill deficits and to determine a starting point for instruction. Do not unnecessarily frustrate the student. In some cases, you may wish to administer the Check Test in sections as the students progress through the book rather than in one sitting.

INTERPRETING RESULTS AND PLANNING INSTRUCTION

Results of students' performances on the Check Test should be recorded on the Accuracy Checklists. A blank Accuracy Checklist is provided on page 68 and at the back of the student's workbook. Record section scores in reading and spelling as a fraction, writing the number read or spelled correctly over the number five. Refer to the sample Accuracy Checklist on page 5.

By examining the Check Test Scores column, it should be readily apparent which list a student should begin work on. If a student reads and spells all words from a particular section correctly, instruction on the corresponding list is not necessary and can be marked "mastered." In this case, the student can immediately begin to build reading proficiency on that list (Step 6). If a student indicates mastery in reading but not in spelling, proceed through the learning steps that focus on the spelling tasks. If a student scores 4/5 for a given list, begin instruction at Step 5, working to increase accuracy. The accuracy check will reveal if additional instruction on Steps 1 through 4 will be necessary. Obviously a student who reads or spells fewer than three words correctly will require more instructional time than a student who has nearly mastered that list.

LIST 9: CONSONANT SUFFIXES AND PLURALS*

-ly, -ty	-ful, -fully	-ment, -ness	-some, -less	Plural -s	Plural -es
badly	careful	apartment	bothersome	airplanes	ashes
completely	carefully	basement	handsome	baskets	babies
finally	cheerful	government	lonesome	blankets	benches
friendly	cheerfully	movement	troublesome	blossoms	bodies
gladly	colorful	pavement	wholesome	bubbles	boxes
hardly	faithful	payment		buttons	branches
lately	faithfully	placement	blameless	cabins	brushes
likely	fearful	shipment	careless	camels	bushes
lonely	fearfully	statement	childless	candles	butterflies
lovely	forceful		endless	farmers	churches
monthly	forcefully	brightness	fearless	fingers	cities
mostly	graceful	darkness	harmless	gardens	classes
namely	gracefully	goodness	helpless	insects	copies
nearly	grateful	happiness	homeless	manners	dishes
nicely	gratefully	illness	lifeless	monkeys	dresses
quickly	hateful	kindness	pointless	needles	glasses
quietly	helpful	likeness	priceless	newspapers	inches
really	hopeful	sadness	restless	notebooks	parties
safely	hopefully	shyness	speechless	persons	peaches
slowly	joyful	sickness	useless	pickles	ponies
surely	painful	soreness	worthless	problems	puppies
swiftly	painfully	stillness		rabbits	sandwiches
widely	playful	weakness		squirrels	stories
yearly	playfully			subjects	studies
	skillful			tables	taxes
ninety	thankful			turkeys	wishes
safety	thankfully			uncles	witches
seventy	truthful			valleys	
sixty	truthfully				
	useful				
	wasteful				
	wonderful				

*All words on this list are practical spelling words. The teacher and student should decide together how many of these words the student will be responsible for spelling.

CONCEPTS

Introduce:

Suffix — A suffix is a word part that is added to the end of a root. Sometimes a suffix changes the meaning of a word (*careless, careful*), and sometimes it changes the way a word is used in a sentence, i.e., its part of speech (*dressing, dressed, dressy*).

Consonant Suffix — A consonant suffix is a suffix that begins with a consonant. The following consonant suffixes are introduced in List 9: *-ly, -ty, -ful, -fully, -ment, -some, -less, -ness.*

Root — A root is the main word part to which suffixes are attached. Roots may be words by themselves (*slowly, unsinkable*), or they may be Latin, Greek, or Anglo-Saxon words that are not real words in the English language (*prefer, depending*).

Spelling Generalization — When adding a consonant suffix to a root, write the root in full and then add the suffix in full (*safe + ly = safely, base + ment = basement*). Usually you do not change the root when adding a consonant suffix.

Plural — A plural is a word form that indicates more than one. *Airplanes* is the plural of *airplane; churches,* of *church; stories,* of *story.*

Spelling Rules for the Formation of Plurals—

- Most of the time, add *-s* to the word to spell its plural (*baskets, uncles*).
- If a word ends in *s, x, z, sh,* or *ch,* add *-es* to spell its plural (*glasses, brushes, churches*). Students do not need to memorize this rule because *-es* adds an extra syllable and can be heard.
- If a word ends in *y* preceded by a consonant, change the *y* to *i* and add *-es* (*pennies, babies*). If the *y* is preceded by a vowel, add *-s (toys, turkeys)*.

LEARNING STEPS

STEP 1. Work with the Isolated Word Parts

Reading — The students will correctly pronounce the isolated suffixes *-ly, -ty, -ful, -fully, -ment, -some, -less,* and *-ness.*

Spelling — The students will spell these suffixes as the teacher dictates them, sounding them aloud while spelling.

Point out that the suffix *-ful* has only one *l* whereas the word *full* ends with two *l*'s. The reason the suffix *-fully* has two *l*'s is that it is a combination of two suffixes: *ful + ly = fully.*

Drill activities for Step 1 (reading and spelling the suffixes in isolation) are ideally done by having students make their own drill cards. Refer to Special Considerations on page 8. Students can work individually or in pairs to practice reading and spelling the suffixes.

STEP 2. Work with the Combined Word Parts

Reading — The students will identify suffixes and then combine them with roots to make words. (See Worksheet 9–A.)

Spelling — The students will spell the suffixes and roots heard in words. (See Worksheet 9–B.)

Dictate the following words for Worksheet 9–B. Make certain that the students repeat the word (*useless*), isolate the root (*use*), and say it aloud while spelling it.

1. useless	2. statement	3. lovely	4. seventy	5. goodness
6. cheerful	7. pavement	8. hopefully	9. restless	10. gladly

For words 11–19, the students will follow the procedures above, except that they will isolate and spell only the suffix.

11. kindness	12. hopeful	13. friendly	14. carefully	15. shipment
16. safety	17. endless	18. lonesome	19. helpful	

STEP 3. Work with the Whole Word

Reading — The students will divide words by separating the suffix from the root. (See Worksheet 9–C.)

Spelling — The students will spell words with consonant suffixes and will apply the rules for forming plurals. (See Worksheets 9–D, 9–E, and 9–F.)

Dictate the following words for the first half of Worksheet 9–F. Make certain that the students repeat each word aloud.

1. helpful	2. sadness	3. really	4. basement	5. hopefully
6. safety	7. useful	8. careless	9. quickly	10. lonesome
11. statement	12. lovely	13. kindness	14. carefully	15. thankful
16. endless				

Dictate the following words for the last half of Worksheet 9–F.

17. branches	18. problems	19. copies	20. ashes	21. stories
22. glasses	23. buttons	24. cities	25. fingers	26. puppies
27. taxes	28. insects			

STEP 4. Work with Words in Context

Meaning — The students will use List 9 words in definitions and in context. (See Worksheets 9–G, 9–H, and 9–I.)

Reading and Spelling — The students will read and write sentences that contain List 9 words. (See Worksheet 9–J.)

Note: Any words that exemplify the principles of the word list may be circled.

STEP 5. Increase Reading and Spelling Accuracy and Monitor Progress

Reading — The students will read ten randomly selected words from List 9 with 90 percent accuracy. Record their progress on the Accuracy Checklists.

Spelling — The students will spell from dictation ten practical spelling words from List 9 with 90 percent accuracy. Record their progress on the Accuracy Checklists.

STEP 6. Build Reading Proficiency, Monitor Progress, and Encourage Spontaneous Writing

Record students' progress on the Proficiency Graphs.

LIST 10: VOWEL SUFFIXES AND SPELLING RULES*

-ing	-er, -est	-en, -ish	-y	Mixed Suffixes Drop-the-e Rule	Doubling and Y Rules
adding	brighter	beaten	cloudy	biting	biggest
asking	brightest	brighten	curly	blamed	bitten
banking	cleaner	dampen	dirty	broken	clipper
barking	cleanest	eaten	eighty	caring	digging
bringing	colder	fallen	healthy	chosen	drummer
buying	coldest	frighten	lucky	dancing	earlier
crying	darker	golden	messy	driven	earliest
dressing	deepest	harden	mighty	frozen	easier
drying	faster	lengthen	rainy	frozen	floppy
falling	fastest	sharpen	risky	icy	funniest
farming	fewer	shorten	rusty	largest	funny
fishing	greater	wooden	sandy	latest	gotten
helping	greatest	woolen	sleepy	leaving	hidden
jumping	higher		snowy	loving	hotter
milking	highest	British	sticky	placing	lazier
packing	longer	foolish	stormy	riding	madder
planting	longest	selfish	tricky	safest	muddy
playing	lowest	Spanish	wealthy	shining	prettiest
printing	nearer		windy	skating	quitting
raining	nearest			sliding	robber
singing	older			smiling	rotten
standing	oldest			smoky	saddest
starting	smaller			stylish	shopping
studying	sooner			taken	sunny
swinging	strongest			tasty	swimming
thinking	warmer			using	wedding
walking	younger			wider	whipping
wanting	youngest			writing	

*All words on List 10 are practical spelling words. The teacher and student should decide together how many of these words the student will be responsible for spelling.

CONCEPTS

Introduce:

Vowel Suffix — A vowel suffix is a suffix that begins with a vowel. The following vowel suffixes are introduced in List 10: *-ing, -er, -est, -ish, -y,* and *-en.*

Spelling Generalization — When adding a vowel suffix to a root, usually write the root in full and then add the suffix in full (*warm + er = warmer, curl + y = curly, wood + en = wooden).* Three major spelling rules are exceptions to this spelling generalization: the Doubling Rule (1-1-1 Rule), the Drop-the-*e* Rule, and the *Y* Rule.

Doubling Rule (1-1-1 Rule) — For one-syllable words ending in one consonant and having one short vowel, double the final consonant before adding a vowel suffix (*sad + est = saddest, plan + ing = planning, rot + en = rotten).* Exception: Never double an *x* (*fixing).*

An alternative explanation of this rule may be easier for some students: When you hear a short-vowel sound in the root, be ready to think. Short vowels must be followed by two consonants in words with suffixes.

- Sometimes you don't need to double the final consonant because there are already two consonants (*planting, oldest, gladly, cupful*).
- Sometimes you need to add another consonant. The double consonant keeps the vowel short (*hopping, runner, funny*).

Drop-the-e Rule — When a root ends in silent *e,* drop the *e* when adding a vowel suffix (*hope + ing = hoping, ice + y = icy, large + er = larger).*

Y Rule — When a root ends in *y,* change the *y* to *i* when adding a suffix (*easy + er = easier, try + ed = tried).*

Exceptions:
- Keep the *y* if it is preceded by a vowel (*play + er = player).*
- Keep the *y* when adding the suffix *-ing (cry + ing = crying).*

Review:

Suffix, Consonant Suffix, Root — See List 9 for definitions.

LEARNING STEPS

STEP 1. Work with the Isolated Word Parts

Reading — The students will correctly pronounce the suffixes *-ing, -er, -est, -ish, -y,* and *-en.*

Spelling — The students will spell List 10 suffixes as the teacher dictates them, sounding them aloud while spelling.

Drill activities for Step 1 are ideally done by having students make their own drill cards. Refer to Special Considerations on page 8.

STEP 2. Work with the Combined Word Parts

Reading — The students will identify suffixes and then combine them with roots to make words. (See Worksheets 10–A and 10–B.)

Spelling — The students will spell the suffixes and roots heard in words. (See Worksheet 10–C.)

Dictate the following words for Worksheet 10–C. Make certain that the students repeat the word (*selfish*), isolate the root (*self*), and say it aloud while spelling it.

1. selfish	2. cleaner	3. swinging	4. lucky	5. shorten
6. highest	7. drying	8. sleepy	9. fallen	10. colder

For words 11–19, the students will follow the procedures above except that they will isolate and spell only the suffix.

11. harden	12. brightest	13. foolish	14. wanting	15. nearer
16. barking	17. golden	18. healthy	19. oldest	

16

STEP 3. Work with the Whole Word

Reading — The students will divide words by separating the suffix from the root. (See Worksheet 10–D.)

Spelling — The students will spell words with vowel suffixes and will apply the three major spelling rules: the Doubling Rule, the Drop-the-*e* Rule, and the *Y* Rule. (See Worksheets 10–E, 10–F, 10–G, 10–H, 10–I, 10–J, and 10–K.)

Dictate the following words for Worksheet 10–K. Make certain that the students repeat each word aloud.

1. rainy	2. bringing	3. higher	4. wooden	5. fastest
6. selfish	7. prettiest	8. hidden	9. fatter	10. writing
11. broken	12. icy	13. digging	14. sunny	15. easier
16. biggest				

STEP 4. Work with Words in Context

Meaning — The students will use List 10 words in definitions and in context. (See Worksheets 10–L and 10–M.)

Reading and Spelling — The students will read and write sentences that contain List 10 words. (See Worksheet 10–N.)

STEP 5. Increase Reading and Spelling Accuracy and Monitor Progress

Reading — The students will read ten randomly selected words from List 10 with 90 percent accuracy. Record their progress on the Accuracy Checklists.

Spelling — The students will spell from dictation ten practical spelling words from List 10 with 90 percent accuracy. Record their progress on the Accuracy Checklists.

STEP 6. Build Reading Proficiency, Monitor Progress, and Encourage Spontaneous Writing

Record students' progress on the Proficiency Graphs.

LIST 11: THREE SOUNDS OF -ed*

/t/	/d/	/ed/	Mixed with Drop-the-e Rule	Mixed with Doubling and Y Rules
asked	called	acted	bored	begged
banked	crawled	added	cared	buried
barked	filled	crowded	carved	carried
brushed	filmed	drifted	caused	clapped
camped	formed	ended	chased	cried
dressed	formed	floated	closed	dried
dumped	happened	folded	created	dropped
fixed	learned	handed	danced	envied
forced	ordered	invented	fired	fried
helped	owned	landed	forced	grabbed
jumped	played	lasted	hired	hurried
kicked	pressed	lifted	joked	married
kissed	pulled	melted	loved	planned
knocked	rained	needed	named	robbed
laughed	rolled	painted	placed	shipped
licked	screamed	planted	raised	shopped
milked	seemed	pointed	saved	skinned
mixed	signed	punted	scared	snapped
packed	smelled	rented	served	spotted
passed	snowed	roasted	shaped	stepped
picked	spelled	rusted	skated	stopped
pumped	spilled	sounded	smiled	studied
rocked	stayed	started	supposed	tried
stamped	trained	tested	tasted	trimmed
stuffed	turned	treated	tired	tripped
thanked	used	twisted	typed	whipped
tricked	watered	waited	united	worried
washed	yelled	wanted	used	wrapped

*All words on List 11 are practical spelling words. The teacher and student should decide together how many of these words the student will be responsible for spelling.

CONCEPTS

Introduce:

-ed Suffix — The suffix *-ed* is usually attached to a verb and places the action in the past tense (Today I plant; yesterday I planted). This vowel suffix can take on three different sounds, (/t/, /d/, and /əd/), depending upon the final sound of the root to which it is attached (*jumped, called, acted*). *-ed* has a fourth, less-common sound, which is discussed in Worksheet 11–E: /ēd/ as in *hurried*.

Review:

Suffix, Root — See List 9 for definitions.
Vowel Suffix, Doubling Rule, Drop-the-e Rule, Y Rule — See List 10 for definitions.
Spelling Generalization — When adding a suffix to a root, write the root in full and then add the suffix in full (*safe + ly = safely, crack + ed = cracked*). It is particularly important that the students repeat the word and the root before spelling words with the suffix *-ed*. They should next spell the root in full. This is especially helpful when they spell words such as *asked* in which the /k/ sound is not easily heard. By saying "ask" first, the students will hear all the sounds and be more likely to spell with accuracy. This procedure is also helpful for words that require students to apply one of the three spelling rules.

LEARNING STEPS

STEP 1. Work with the Isolated Word Parts

Reading — The students will correctly pronounce the three sounds of *-ed* as /t/, /d/, and /əd/.

Spelling — The students will spell the sound of:
/əd/ as *ed*
/t/ as *ed*
/d/ as *ed*

STEP 2. Work with the Combined Word Parts

Reading — The students will identify the suffix *-ed* and the root in a group of words. (See Worksheet 11–A.)

Spelling — The students will practice spelling the three sounds of *-ed*. (See Worksheets 11–B and 11–C.)

Dictate the following words for the last half of Worksheet 11–B. Make certain that the students repeat the word, isolate the root, and say it aloud while spelling it.

1. snowed	2. formed	3. barked	4. rented	5. dressed
6. sounded	7. tricked	8. rolled	9. pointed	10. failed

Dictate the following words for the last half of Worksheet 11–C. Students will isolate and spell the suffix.

1. pumped	2. sadness	3. smelled	4. acted	5. falling
6. played	7. likely	8. washed		

STEP 3. Work with the Whole Word

Reading — The students will read words that contain the suffix *-ed*. (See Worksheet 11–D.)

Spelling — The students will spell words with suffixes and will apply the three major spelling rules: the Doubling Rule, the Drop-the-e Rule, and the Y Rule. (See Worksheets 11–D, 11–E, 11–F, and 11–G.)

Dictate the following words for the last half of Worksheet 11–D. Make certain that the students say the root aloud first.

1. banked	2. asked	3. gladly	4. watered	5. safety
6. tested	7. shapeless	8. dumped		

STEP 4. Work with Words in Context

Meaning — The students will use List 11 words in definitions and in context. (See Worksheet 11–H.)

Reading and Spelling — The students will read and write sentences that contain List 11 words. (See Worksheets 11–I and 11–J.)

STEP 5. Increase Reading and Spelling Accuracy and Monitor Progress

Reading — The students will read ten randomly selected words from List 11 with 90 percent accuracy. Record their progress on the Accuracy Checklists.

Spelling — The students will spell from dictation ten practical spelling words from List 11 with 90 percent accuracy. Record their progress on the Accuracy Checklists.

STEP 6. Build Reading Proficiency, Monitor Progress, and Encourage Spontaneous Writing

Record students' progress on the Proficiency Graphs.

LIST 12: SPELLING PATTERNS–VOWEL SUFFIXES

bated	hater	rated	snipper
batted	hatter	ratted	snipping
bidding	hidden	ridding	spiting
biding	hiding	riding	spitting
caning	* hoped	riper	* staring
canning	* hopped	ripper	starring
cuter	* hoping	robbed	stilled
cutter	* hopping	robed	striped
diner	mating	* scared	stripped
* dinner	matting	scarred	styled
doted	moping	scarring	taped
dotted	mopping	* scary	taping
filed	pined	scraper	tapped
* filled	pinned	scrapper	tapping
* filling	planed	sloping	wiled
filing	* planned	* sloppy	willed
griping	planing	sniper	
gripping	* planning	sniping	

*Practical spelling words. The teacher and student should decide together how many of these words the student will be responsible for spelling.

CONCEPTS

Introduce:

Spelling Generalization — A short-vowel sound in the first syllable of a word that has a suffix must be followed by two consonants. Therefore, students must remember to double the middle consonant when a single consonant sound is heard between two vowels (*sloppy, cutter*). If a long-vowel sound is heard in the first syllable of a word with a suffix, only one consonant will follow it (*sloping, cuter*).

An alternative procedure for teaching the spelling of List 12 words is to train students to apply the Doubling Rule (*hop* becomes *hopping*) or the Drop-the-*e* Rule (*hope* becomes *hoping*) as described in List 10. This is perhaps the more common approach. However, we have found that most students are more successful in reading and spelling these words if they identify the first vowel sound as short or long. If the first vowel is short, it must be followed by two consonants; if the first vowel is long, only one consonant will follow.

Review:

Closed and Open Syllables — See *Megawords 1* for definitions.
VC/CV Syllabication Rule and *V/CV Syllabication Rule* — See *Megawords 1* for definitions.
Suffix and Root — See List 9 for definitions.

LEARNING STEPS

STEP 1. Work with the Isolated Word Parts

Reading and Spelling — The students will correctly read and spell closed and open syllables. (See Worksheet 12-A.)

Dictate the following syllables for the last half of Worksheet 12-A:

1. ta	2. spi	3. bid	4. mop	5. stri
6. mo	7. cu	8. slap	9. dot	10. slop
11. ho	12. scar	13. rat	14. fi	15. ba

STEP 2. Work with the Combined Word Parts

Reading — The students will pronounce word parts and combine them to make a whole word. (See Worksheet 12-B.)

Dictionaries divide words that drop the *e* when a vowel suffix is added just before the suffix (*hop·ing, cut·er*). However, such words in List 12 are divided between the first vowel and the following consonant so that the long vowel occurs in an open syllable (*ho·ping, cu·ter*).
Spelling — The students will isolate, pronounce, and spell parts of dictated words. (See Worksheet 12-C.)

For the first half of Worksheet 12-C, the students will spell the first part of the following words:

1. taping	2. ratted	3. scraper	4. matting	5. snipping
6. diner	7. griping	8. sloppy	9. batted	10. filing

For the last half of Worksheet 12-C, the students will identify the middle consonant or consonants in the following words:

1. riper	2. planning	3. gripping	4. sloping	5. rated
6. staring	7. pinned	8. hiding	9. hopped	10. pined

STEP 3. Work with the Whole Word

Reading — The students will identify the root and then pronounce the whole word. (See Worksheet 12-D.)

Spelling — The students will repeat and spell words according to their spelling patterns. (See Worksheet 12-E.)

For the middle part of Worksheet 12-E, dictate the following words. Make certain that the students repeat the word aloud and identify the first vowel as long or short before they begin spelling.

1. tubing	2. griped	3. tubby	4. hoping	5. gripping
6. cuter	7. hopped	8. scarred	9. cutting	10. scared
11. diner	12. dinner			

STEP 4. Work with Words in Context

Meaning — The students will use List 12 words in definitions and in context. (See Worksheet 12–F.)

Reading and Spelling — The students will read and write sentences that contain List 12 words. (See Worksheet 12-G.)

STEP 5. Increase Reading and Spelling Accuracy and Monitor Progress

Reading — The students will read ten randomly selected words from List 12 with 90 percent accuracy. Record their progress on the Accuracy Checklists.

Spelling — The students will spell from dictation ten practical spelling words from List 12 with 90 percent accuracy. Record their progress on the Accuracy Checklists.

STEP 6. Build Reading Proficiency, Monitor Progress, and Encourage Spontaneous Writing

Record students' progress on the Proficiency Graphs.

LIST 13: COMMON PREFIXES

re- (back, again)	de- (down, away from)	sub- (below, under) pro- (forward)	pre- (before) per- (through, completely)	un- (not) in- (not, in)	ex- (out)
* rebuild	* decide	* subject	* prepare	* unable	* exact
* receive	* defeat	* subtract	* present	* unfair	* exam
* recess	* defend	sublet	* present	* unfinished	* except
* recite	* delight	submarine	predict	* unfriendly	* exchange
* record	* department	submerge	prefer	* unkind	* excite
* refuse	* depend	submit	prefix	* unknown	* excuse
* rejoice	* deposit	subscribe	prenatal	unborn	* exit
* remain	* describe	subsist	prepaid		* expect
* remind	* deserve	subsoil	preschool	* income	* explain
* remove	* desire	substance	prescribe	* inform	* explore
* repair	* destroy	subway	preside	* inside	* express
* repeat	debate	subzero	pretend	* insult	* extra
* repel	decrease		preview	* intend	exceed
* report	defect	* produce		* invent	exclude
* respect	defer	* program	* perfect	inboard	exempt
* return	deform	* project	* perfume	incorrect	exhaust
* review	degrade	* promise	* perhaps	increase	exist
* reward	demand	* protect	* permit	indent	expand
recall	demote	proceed	perform	indirect	expel
refill	depart	proclaim	perplex	inept	expert
reform	depress	product	persist	inflate	expire
refresh	descend	profile	perspire	inhale	explode
refuel		profit	persuade	inscribe	export
regain		progress	pertain	insert	expose
regard		promote	perturb	insist	extend
reject		propel	peruse	inspect	extreme
resist		prospect	pervade	inspire	
		prosper		intake	
		provide			

*Practical spelling words. The teacher and student should decide together how many of these words the student will be responsible for spelling.

CONCEPTS

Introduce:

Prefix — A prefix is a word part that comes before a root and changes its meaning or forms a new word (*unpaid, prepaid, decrease, increase*).

re- = back, again	*ex-* = out
de- = down, away from	*pre-* = before
sub- = below, under	*pro-* = forward
in- = not, in	*per-* = through, completely
un- = not	

Accent Patterns — A student's ability to recognize multisyllabic words often depends upon ability to accent the proper syllable. Following are some general guidelines for accenting two-syllable words.

1. Accent on the first syllable (_____ ' _____)
   Most two-syllable words have the accent on the first syllable (*fi' nal, stu' dent, hop' ping*).
2. Accent on the second syllable (_____ _____ ')
   Two-syllable words that are accented on the second syllable usually have a prefix in the first syllable and a root in the second syllable (*ex tend', con fuse'*).
3. Accent on either the first or second syllable (_____' _____ or _____ _____')
   If a word can function as both a noun and a verb, the noun form will have the accent on the prefix (*sub' ject*) and the verb form will have the accent on the root (*sub ject'*).

Review:

Root — A root is the main word part to which prefixes and suffixes are attached. Roots may be words by themselves (*repay, disobey*) or they may be Latin, Greek, or Anglo-Saxon words that are not real words in the English language (*prefer, depend*).

Accented Syllable — An accented syllable is pronounced as if it were a one-syllable word having a clear vowel sound according to its syllabic type (*ac' tive, com plete'* , *ser' vant, loy' al*).

Unaccented Syllable — An unaccented syllable is pronounced with a schwa /ə/ or short-*i* vowel sound regardless of its syllabic type (*rib' bon, i mag' ine, doc' tor*).

LEARNING STEPS

STEP 1. Work with the Isolated Word Parts

Reading — The students will correctly pronounce the isolated prefixes *re-, de-, sub-, pro-, pre-, per-, un-, in-,* and *ex-*.

Spelling — The students will spell these prefixes as they are dictated by the teacher, sounding them aloud while spelling.

Meaning — The students will identify the meaning of each prefix and give an example of a word for each. (See Worksheets 13–A and 13–B.)

Drill activities for Step 1 are ideally done by having students make their own drill cards. Refer to Special Considerations on page 8. Students can work individually or in pairs to practice the reading, spelling, and meanings of the prefixes.

STEP 2. Work with the Combined Word Parts

Reading — The students will identify prefixes and combine them with roots to make words. (See Worksheet 13–C.)

Spelling — The students will isolate, pronounce, and spell first the prefix and then the root heard in each dictated word. (See Worksheet 13–D.)

Dictate words 1–10. Make certain that the students repeat the sample word (*subject*), isolate the prefix (*sub-*), and say it aloud while spelling.

1. proceed	2. excuse	3. prepaid	4. respect	5. inhale
6. unable	7. substance	8. descend	9. exclude	10. persuade

Dictate words 11–20. The students will repeat the sample word (*expect*), isolate the root (*pect*), and say it aloud while spelling.

11. intake	12. perform	13. submit	14. predict	15. program
16. extreme	17. decrease	18. refresh	19. extend	20. perspire

Caution the students about spelling words with *ex-*. They will be tempted to insert the letter *s* because the sound of *ex-* is /eks/. Tell them that *ex-* is (for all practical purposes) *never* followed by an *s*. (Who ever spells the words *exsertile* or *exstipulate*?!)

Meaning — The students will apply their knowledge of the meanings of prefixes to make words with prefixes. (See Worksheets 13–E and 13–F.)

STEP 3. Work with the Whole Word

Reading — The students will separate the prefix from the root and practice accent patterns in two-syllable words. (See Worksheets 13–G and 13–H.)

Worksheets 13–G and 13–H include words that can be divided in two ways: 1) into prefixes and roots *(pro/spect)* and 2) into syllables according to the VC/CV or VC/V Syllabication Rules *(pros/pect)*. Discuss these two types of word division. On Worksheet 13–H discuss the starred words, in which syllabication differs depending on whether the word is a noun or a verb.

Spelling — The students will spell practical spelling words that contain prefixes and suffixes. (See Worksheet 13–I.)

Dictate the following words. Make certain that the students repeat each syllable aloud while spelling.

1. unable	2. deserve	3. remind	4. perfume	5. expect
6. intend	7. perfect	8. prevent	9. protect	10. exit

Meaning — The students will use prefixes and roots to form words. (See Worksheet 13–J.)

You may wish to challenge students by seeing if they can determine the meanings of the following words. This is an oral language exercise in which you read the words aloud for the students.

reiterate	submarine	unusual	exterminate
relapse	subliminal	unoccupied	exclusive
renegotiate	subsonic	untouchable	excessive
replete	subordinate	unorganized	exaggerate
resonant	subterfuge	demerit	independent
resilient	percolate	degenerate	indignant
resurrection	perpetual	deteriorate	incurable
propensity	permeate	decarbonate	informal
propaganda	persevere	decelerate	infinite
protrude	perspective	demobilize	

STEP 4. Work with Words in Context

Meaning — The students will use List 13 words in definitions and in context. (See Worksheets 13–K and 13–L.)

Reading and Spelling — The students will read and write sentences that contain List 13 words. (See Worksheet 13–M.)

STEP 5. Increase Reading and Spelling Accuracy and Monitor Progress

Reading — The students will read ten randomly selected words from List 13 with 90 percent accuracy. Record their progress on the Accuracy Checklists.

Spelling — The students will spell from dictation ten practical spelling words from List 13 with 90 percent accuracy. Record their progress on the Accuracy Checklists.

STEP 6. Build Reading Proficiency, Monitor Progress, and Encourage Spontaneous Writing

Record students' progress on the Proficiency Graphs.

LIST 14: ADDITIONAL COMMON PREFIXES

a- (on, in)	dis- (apart, opposite of) mis- (wrong, bad)	ad- (to, toward) trans- (across)	ab- (away from) con- (with, together)	ob- (in the way, against) inter- (between, among)
* about	* discover	* address	* absent	* object
* above	* disease	* admire	abduct	oblong
* across	* dislike	adapt	abhor	obscene
* afar	* dismiss	addict	abort	obscure
* ahead	* distant	adept	absolve	observe
* alive	disabled	adhere	absorb	obsess
* aloud	discard	adjoin	abstain	obstruct
* among	disclose	adjust	abstract	obtain
* asleep	discount	admit	absurd	obtuse
* awake	discuss	advance		
* awhile	disgrace		* conclude	* interest
aback	disgust	* transport	* conduct	* interrupt
aboard	disperse	transact	* connect	interact
adrift	distract	transcend	* contain	intercede
afire		transcribe	* contest	interchange
afloat	* mischief	transfer	* control	interface
agree	* misspell	transform	confer	interfere
alert	* mistake	translate	confess	interject
aloof	misgive	transmit	confuse	interlock
arise	mislead	transplant	consist	interlude
ashore	mismatch		conspire	intersect
aside	misplace		consult	
await	misprint		contract	
	misquote		convict	
			convince	

*Practical spelling words. The teacher and student should decide together how many of these words the student will be responsible for spelling.

CONCEPTS

Review:

Prefix — A prefix is a word part that comes before a root and changes its meaning or forms a new word (*unpaid, prepaid, decrease, increase*).

The following prefixes are introduced in List 14:

a-	= on, in	*trans-*	= across
dis-	= apart, opposite of	*inter-*	= between, among
mis-	= wrong, bad	*con-*	= with, together
ad-	= to, toward	*ob-*	= in the way, against, near
ab-	= away from		

Root — A root is the main word part to which prefixes and suffixes are attached. Roots may be words by themselves (*repay, disobey*) or they may be Latin, Greek, or Anglo-Saxon words that are not real words in the English language (*prefer, depend*).

Accented Syllable — An accented syllable is pronounced as if it were a one-syllable word having a clear vowel sound according to its syllabic type (*ac' tive, com plete', ser' vant, loy' al*).

Unaccented Syllable — An unaccented syllable is pronounced with a schwa /ə/ or short-*i* vowel sound regardless of its syllabic type (*rib' bon, i mag' ine, doc' tor*).

Accent Patterns — A student's ability to recognize multisyllabic words often depends upon ability to accent the proper syllable. Following are some general guidelines for accenting two-syllable words.

1. Accent on the first syllable (_____ ' _____)
   Most two-syllable words have the accent on the first syllable (*fi' nal, stu' dent, hop' ping*).
2. Accent on the second syllable (_____ _____ ')
   Two-syllable words that are accented on the second syllable usually have a prefix in the first syllable and a root in the second syllable (*ex tend', con fuse'*).
3. Accent on either the first or second syllable (_____ ' _____ or _____ _____ ')
   If a word can function as both a noun and a verb, the noun form will have the accent on the prefix (*sub' ject*) and the verb form will have the accent on the root (*sub ject'*).

LEARNING STEPS

STEP 1. Work with the Isolated Word Parts

Reading — The students will correctly pronounce the isolated prefixes *a-, dis-, mis-, ad-, trans-, ab-, inter-, ob-,* and *con-*.

Spelling — The students will spell the List 14 prefixes as they are dictated, sounding them aloud while spelling.

Meaning — The students will identify the meaning of each prefix and give an example of a word for each. (See Worksheets 14–A and 14–B.)

Students should complete these worksheets only after sufficient drill has been done with the prefix cards.

STEP 2. Work with the Combined Word Parts

Reading — The students will identify prefixes and combine them with roots to make words. (See Worksheet 14–C.)

Spelling — The students will isolate, pronounce, and spell the prefix and then the root in dictated words. (See Worksheet 14–D.)

Dictate the following words. Students repeat the word (*misplace*), isolate the prefix (*mis-*), and say it aloud while spelling.

1. misplace	2. transfer	3. interrupt	4. conspire	5. abrupt
6. observe	7. aware	8. disagree	9. address	10. conduct

29

Dictate words 11–20 and have students respond as above except that they spell only the roots.

11. al<u>oud</u>	12. trans<u>act</u>	13. cond<u>uct</u>	14. abs<u>ent</u>	15. dis<u>own</u>
16. ad<u>opt</u>	17. ob<u>tain</u>	18. mis<u>spell</u>	19. dis<u>cover</u>	20. ad<u>mire</u>

Teach the following spelling principle: When you spell words that contain prefixes, write both the prefix and the root in full. Thus, *mis + spell = misspell* and *inter + rupt = interrupt*.

Meaning — The students will apply their knowledge of the meanings of prefixes to make words. (See Worksheet 14–E.)

STEP 3. Work with the Whole Word

Reading — The students will separate the prefix from the root and practice accent patterns in two-syllable words. (See Worksheets 14–F and 14–G.)

Spelling — The students will spell practical spelling words that contain prefixes and suffixes. (See Worksheet 14–H.)

Dictate the following words. Make certain that the students repeat each syllable aloud while spelling.

1. ahead	2. discover	3. contest	4. absent	5. object
6. conclude	7. mistake	8. interrupt	9. transport	10. admire

Meaning — The students will use their knowledge of prefixes to define words that contain prefixes and Latin roots. (See Worksheets 14–I and 14–J.)

You may wish to challenge students to see if they can determine the meanings of the following words. This is an oral language exercise in which you read the words aloud for the students.

condensation	obsolete	international	misinform
confederate	obstinate	intermission	misrepresent
confidence	obnoxious	interdependent	miscarriage
conjunction	obtrusive	interception	misfortune
congregation	obvious	intermarry	abrasive
conception	dissemble	intermittent	abnormal
transistor	disassociate	advocate	abdicate
translucent	disintegrate	administer	abolition
transmission	disparity		
transparent			

STEP 4. Work with Words in Context

Meaning — The students will use List 14 words in definitions and in context. (See Worksheets 14–K and 14–L.)

Reading and Spelling — The students will read and write sentences that contain List 14 words. (See Worksheet 14–M.)

STEP 5. Increase Reading and Spelling Accuracy and Monitor Progress

Reading — The students will read ten randomly selected words from List 14 with 90 percent accuracy. Record their progress on the Accuracy Checklists.

Spelling — The students will spell from dictation ten practical spelling words from List 14 with 90 percent accuracy. Record their progress on the Accuracy Checklists.

STEP 6. Build Reading Proficiency, Monitor Progress, and Encourage Spontaneous Writing

Record students' progress on the Proficiency Graphs.

REVIEW: LISTS 9–14

* awhile	* hired	* reward	* worried	interfere
* biggest	* hopefully	* scared	abstain	interject
* blankets	* invent	* shorten	abstract	mislead
* brightest	* kicked	* sloppy	adapt	misplace
* cried	* ordered	* soreness	addict	mopping
* dancing	* painted	* spilled	ashore	obscure
* describe	* peaches	* stamped	bitten	perform
* dried	* persons	* stories	consult	perturb
* easier	* placing	* studying	convict	prescribe
* foolish	* pointless	* styled	decrease	profile
* frozen	* ponies	* swinging	discard	scraper
* glasses	* priceless	* tasted	discount	striped
* grateful	* quietly	* trimmed	explode	submerge
* greater	* really	* unfinished	filed	submit
* happened	* refuse	* used	griping	transfer
* helping	* rented	* wealthy	insist	transplant

* Practical spelling words. The teacher and student should decide together how many of these words the student will be responsible for spelling.

LEARNING STEPS

For the Review List, only Steps 5 and 6 are applicable.

STEP 5. Increase Reading and Spelling Accuracy and Monitor Progress

Reading — The students will read ten randomly selected words from the Review List with 90 percent accuracy and record their progress on the Accuracy Checklists.

Spelling — The students will spell from dictation ten practical spelling words from the Review List with 90 percent accuracy and record their progress on the Accuracy Checklists.

STEP 6. Build Reading Proficiency, Monitor Progress, and Encourage Spontaneous Writing

Students record their progress on the Proficiency Graphs.

ANSWERS

WORKSHEET 9–A

A **suffix** is a word part that comes at the end of a word. Sometimes it changes the meaning of a word (*careful, careless*) and sometimes it changes the way the word is used in a sentence, i.e., its part of speech (*dressing, dressed, dressy*).

A **root** is the main word part to which suffixes are attached (*slowly, unsinkable*).
A **consonant suffix** is a suffix that begins with a consonant. Learn to recognize these consonant suffixes: *-ly, -ty, -ful, -fully, -ment, -some, -less,* and *-ness.*
Do not change the root when adding a consonant suffix.

Circle the suffixes in the following words.

skil**ful**	point**less**	govern**ment**	sick**ness**
nice**ly**	lone**some**	faith**fully**	hand**some**
move**ment**	safe**ly**	blame**less**	nine**ty**
truth**fully**	sore**ness**	grace**ful**	wide**ly**

Match each root with a suffix to make a real word. Then say the word as you write it.

safe — ty / ment / less = **safety**

shy — ty / ness / ment = **shyness**

color — ness / ful / ly / some = **colorful**

fear — ly / ment / fully = **fearfully**

thank — ful / ly = **thankful**

use — some / ty / less = **useless**

whole — some / ness / ful / ty / fully = **wholesome**

base — ful / ment / ty = **basement**

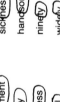
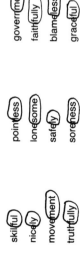

2

WORKSHEET 9–B

Your teacher will dictate some words. Repeat each word, isolate the root, and spell it. Then write the whole word, saying it aloud as you spell.

	Root		Copy	ABC Order
1.	use	+ less =	useless	cheerfully
2.	state	+ ment =	statement	gladly
3.	love	+ ly =	lovely	goodness
4.	seven	+ ty =	seventy	hopefully
5.	good	+ ness =	goodness	lovely
6.	cheer	+ ful =	cheerful	pavement
7.	pave	+ ment =	pavement	restless
8.	hope	+ fully =	hopefully	seventy
9.	rest	+ less =	restless	statement
10.	glad	+ ly =	gladly	useless

Your teacher will dictate some more words. Repeat each word, isolate the suffix, and spell it. Then write the whole word, saying it aloud as you spell.

	Suffix		Copy	ABC Order
11. kind	+	ness	= kindness	carefully
12. hope	+	ful	= hopeful	endless
13. friend	+	ly	= friendly	friendly
14. care	+	fully	= carefully	helpful
15. ship	+	ment	= shipment	hopeful
16. safe	+	ty	= safety	kindness
17. end	+	less	= endless	lonesome
18. lone	+	some	= lonesome	safety
19. help	+	ful	= helpful	shipment

Now go back and write the words in each section in alphabetical order.

3

In the following words, draw a line between the root and the suffix. Then pronounce each word as you write the root and suffix on the first two lines and the whole word on the third line.

	Root	Suffix	Word
lone|some	lone	some	lonesome
swiftly	swift	ly	swiftly
carefully	care	fully	carefully
pavement	pave	ment	pavement
really	real	ly	really
priceless	price	less	priceless
completely	complete	ly	completely
soreness	sore	ness	soreness
basement	base	ment	basement
finally	final	ly	finally
wonderful	wonder	ful	wonderful

Unscramble the words and spell them correctly in the blanks. They all contain suffixes. The meanings and first letters are your clues to arranging the letters in the correct order.

1. ahluftnk   thankful   full of thanks
2. ywsoll   slowly   not quickly
3. seldesn   endless   never ending
4. slestnlis   stillness   total quiet
5. eiynnt   ninety   comes after 89
6. cepshessel   speechless   unable to speak

Review: A suffix is a word part that comes at the end of a word.

A consonant suffix is a suffix that begins with a consonant.

A root is the main word part to which suffixes are attached.

4

Most of the time, add *s* to a word to make it plural. But if a word ends in *s*, *sh*, *ch*, *z* or *x*, add *es* to make it plural.

Add *es* or *s* to the following words to make them plural. Notice that adding *es* adds another syllable to the word, but adding *s* does not change the number of syllables.

boxes	boxes	uncles	uncles
camels	camels	churches	churches
inches	inches	dresses	dresses
farmers	farmers	brushes	brushes
peaches	peaches	tables	tables
classes	classes	squirrels	squirrels
manners	manners	wishes	wishes
taxes	taxes	sandwiches	sandwiches
benches	benches	blankets	blankets
bubbles	bubbles	dishes	dishes
witches	witches	glasses	glasses

Find and circle all of the words above in the puzzle below. The words can be found in a straight line across or up and down.

5

WORKSHEET 9–F

Your teacher will dictate words that have suffixes. Spell them under the correct heading.

-ly	-ful	-fully
really	helpful	hopefully
quickly	useful	carefully
lovely	thankful	

-ment	-less	-ness
basement	careless	sadness
statement	endless	kindness

-ty	-some	
safety	lonesome	

Your teacher will dictate plural words. Decide which rule to apply and spell the words under the correct headings.

Add s	Add es	Change y to i and add es
problems	branches	copies
buttons	ashes	stories
fingers	glasses	cities
insects	taxes	puppies

Proofing Practice: Two common List 9 words are misspelled in each of the sentences below. Correct them as shown.

1. When the train ~~finaly~~ finally arrived, it was ~~ninty~~ ninety minutes late.
2. We were very ~~greatful~~ grateful for the ~~hansome~~ handsome gift.
3. It is hard to be ~~chearful~~ cheerful when the ~~goverment~~ government is at war.
4. New York has more ~~newspapers~~ newspapers than most ~~sitties~~ cities.
5. The ~~playfull~~ playful children never walk down the halls ~~queitly~~ quietly.

7

WORKSHEET 9–E

If a word ends in y with a consonant just before it, change the y to i and add es to make the word plural (city——→cities).
If a word ends in y with a vowel before it, add s (valley——→valleys; boy——→boys; play——→plays).

Circle the letter just before the y. Then spell the plurals of these words.

	Plural	ABC Order
stud(y)	studies	babies
turk(e)y	turkeys	bodies
part(y)	parties	butterflies
bab(y)	babies	copies
cop(y)	copies	ladies
pon(y)	ponies	monkeys
stor(y)	stories	parties
vall(e)y	valleys	ponies
lad(y)	ladies	puppies
bod(y)	bodies	stories
pupp(y)	puppies	studies
monk(e)y	monkeys	turkeys
butterfl(y)	butterflies	valleys

Now go back and write the words in alphabetical order.

Review: To make a word that ends in vowel-y plural, add s.

To make a word that ends in consonant-y plural, change the y to i and add es.

6

Adding the suffix *-ness* to a root that is an adjective (describing word) changes it to a noun (naming word). Add the suffix *-ness* to each root. Then write the noun in the right sentence.

good n e s s   sad a e s s   sick n e s s   still n e s s

bright n e s s   dark n e s s   weak n e s s

1. The ___brightness___ of the floodlights blinded her for a minute.

2. Francis was upset by the death of his pet. You could see the ___sadness___ in his face.

3. Jan missed school last week because of ___sickness___.

4. The ___darkness___ of the night and the howl of a lone wolf frightened us.

5. My grandma is so funny. She always says, "My ___goodness___, won't we have a lark!"

6. Because of a ___weakness___ in his back, Mr. Palmer cannot lift anything heavy.

7. In the middle of the hurricane there was a period of eerie ___stillness___.

Adding the suffix *-less* to a root that is a noun (naming word) changes it to an adjective (describing word). Add the suffix *-less* to each root. Then write the adjective in the right sentence.

worth l e s s   use l e s s   rest l e s s

life l e s s   fear l e s s   care l e s s

8. Megan did not sleep well. She spent a ___restless___ night.

9. Yesterday Donald was arrested because he wrote ten ___worthless___ checks.

10. The party was no fun at all. It was completely ___lifeless___.

11. I have no idea what to do with this gift. The Bartons always give ___useless___ gifts.

12. The ___fearless___ children went rock climbing every weekend.

13. Tracy missed number seven on the grammar quiz. She made a ___careless___ mistake.

9

The suffix *-ful* changes the root from a noun (naming word) to an adjective (describing word). The suffix *-fully* changes the root to an adverb (a word that describes action). Read the sentences and write the word with the correct suffix in each blank.

1. grace   Coretta dances ___gracefully___. She is a
           (adverb)
           ___graceful___ person.
           (adjective)

2. care   Be ___careful___! You must wash the china very
           (adjective)
           ___carefully___.
           (adverb)

3. thank   Sandy was ___thankful___ for all of the gifts.
           (adjective)

4. hope   "Things will work out for the best," she said ___hopefully___.
           (adverb)

5. pain   Carlos ___painfully___ moved his right leg.
           (adverb)

6. help   Children should learn how to be ___helpful___ around the
           (adjective)
           house.

7. color   The leaves are ___colorful___ this time of year.
           (adjective)

8. cheer   Shawn always works ___cheerfully___.
           (adverb)

9. skill   Linda is ___skillful___ at her job.
           (adjective)

10. hate   Milton was so mad that he was ___hateful___ toward everyone.
           (adjective)

11. play   The kitten ___playfully___ chased the ball of string.
           (adverb)

12. fear   Terry ___fearfully___ pulled the trigger of the gun.
           (adverb)

13. faith   Odysseus' ___faithful___ wife waited for him for over
           (adjective)
           twenty years.

14. waste   It is ___wasteful___ to throw away aluminum cans when we
           (adjective)
           can recycle them.

Review: A ___noun___ is a naming word. An ___adjective___ is a describing word. An ___adverb___ describes action.

8

WORKSHEET 9–I

Fill in each blank with one of these suffixes so that the sentence makes sense.

-some   -ly   -ty   -ment

1. I will glad _ly_ help you if I can.
2. Marvin is very good-looking. I think he is quite hand _some_.
3. Have you made your last pay _ment_ on the loan?
4. There should be no move _ment_ when I try to take your picture.
5. It isn't like _ly_ that you could read that entire book in one evening.
6. I don't like to be by myself all weekend. I get lone _some_ for company.
7. When there is snow on the pave _ment_, the children rollerskate in our base _ment_.
8. Donna is still looking for a job. She would like to work for the state govern _ment_.
9. After nine _ty_ days on the job, I am final _ly_ getting the hang of it.
10. We had to move from our apart _ment_ when the landlord raised our rent by seven _ty_ dollars.
11. Mr. Gibbons ate only whole _some_ foods: nuts, berries, fruit, and grains.
12. Ms. Wisty makes a month _ly_ payment on her car.
13. The fearless raccoons were very bother _some_ when they raided our food pack at night.

Copy the words that have suffixes under the correct headings.

-some	-ly	-ty	-ment
handsome	gladly	ninety	payment
lonesome	likely	seventy	movement
wholesome	finally		pavement
bothersome	monthly		basement
			government
			apartment

10

WORKSHEET 9–J

Read the following sentences and circle all the List 9 words that you can find.

1. Three (squirrels) ran (playfully) around the (bushes)
2. (Babies) are (completely) (helpless)
3. (Newspapers) in large (cities) are (widely) read by many (persons)
4. Although Alan seemed (cheerful) and (friendly) he (really) was (lonesome) for his family.
5. (Lately) the children have been (careless) about their (manners)
6. Martha is (careful) to keep the (playful) (puppies) in the (basement)
7. (Churches) do not have to pay (taxes) to the (government)
8. In the (stillness) of the night, Agnes (quietly) read two short (stories)
9. The (blossoms) on the (branches) are (lovely) this spring.
10. It is (useless) and (wasteful) to make so many (copies) of that (statement)
11. The (graceful) (dancers) waited (hopefully) for the results of the tryout.

Take out a piece of blank paper. Your teacher will dictate three of the sentences above for you to write.

Sentences – Teacher corrected.

Now select ten words from List 9 and create a short story or a descriptive paragraph that uses those words. Be creative and avoid repetition!

_____

Reading Accuracy: Demonstrate your accuracy in reading and spelling List 9 words. Your teacher will select ten words to read and ten practical spelling words for you to spell. Record your scores on the Accuracy Checklist. Work toward 90–100 percent accuracy.

Reading Proficiency: Now build up your reading fluency with List 9 words. Decide on your rate goal with your teacher. Record your progress on the Proficiency Graph.

My goal for reading List 9 is _____ words per minute with two or fewer errors.

11

A **vowel suffix** is a suffix that begins with a vowel. Learn to recognize these vowel suffixes: -ing, -er, -est, -ish, -y, and -en.

Circle the suffixes in the following words. Be careful; what looks like a suffix may really be part of a root. You should have a complete word left over if you have circled a suffix.

lift(ing)	soft(en)	wren	self(ish)
spring	neat(er)	sleep(y)	squish
low(est)	guest	dark(er)	ring(ing)
dirt(y)	study(ing)	prefer	swing

Match each root with a suffix to make a real word. Then say the word as you write it.

think — en / y / ing   _thinking_

slow — est / en / y   _slowest_

sing — est / en / y / ing   _singing_

fool — ish / est / en   _foolish_

beat — est / en / y   _beaten_

gold — er / en / ing   _golden_

Make two words out of the roots and suffixes below.

talk — ing / en / est / er / y   _talking_ _talker_

length — en / est / er / y   _lengthen_ _lengthy_

clean — y / er / est   _cleaner_ _cleanest_

A **consonant suffix** is a suffix that begins with a consonant. -ly, -ty, -ful, -fully, -ment, -some, -less, and -ness are consonant suffixes.

A **vowel suffix** is a suffix that begins with a vowel. The vowel suffixes in List 10 are -ing, -er, -est, -ish, -y, and -en.

Circle at least twelve suffixes in the phrases and sentences below.

Cordless Lighted Visor Mirror
Instantly Fits Any Make Car!

Warning: The Surgeon General Has Determined That Cigarette Smoking Is Dangerous to Your Health.

Try
a little
tenderness

Delightfully Daring...

An Investment
Stainless Steel

Golden Gifts

DINING DISCOVERIES

There's a world waiting to be discovered!

A HEALTHY NEW BODY

a useful black hole

List three consonant suffixes and three vowel suffixes that you circled.

Consonant Suffixes	Vowel Suffixes
less (fully)	ing
ment (ness)	en
ly (ful)	y

WORKSHEET 10-C

Your teacher will dictate some words. Repeat each word, isolate the root, and spell it. Then write the whole word, saying it aloud as you spell.

	Root			Copy		ABC Order
1.	self	+ ish	=	selfish		cleaner
2.	clean	+ er	=	cleaner		colder
3.	swing	+ ing	=	swinging		drying
4.	luck	+ y	=	lucky		fallen
5.	short	+ en	=	shorten		highest
6.	high	+ est	=	highest		lucky
7.	dry	+ ing	=	drying		selfish
8.	sleep	+ y	=	sleepy		shorten
9.	fall	+ en	=	fallen		sleepy
10.	cold	+ er	=	colder		swinging

Isolate, pronounce, and spell the suffix you hear in the words your teacher dictates. Then write the whole word, saying it aloud as you spell.

		Suffix		Copy		ABC Order
11.	hard +	en	=	harden		barking
12.	bright +	est	=	brightest		brightest
13.	fool +	ish	=	foolish		foolish
14.	want +	ing	=	wanting		golden
15.	near +	er	=	nearer		harden
16.	bark +	ing	=	barking		healthy
17.	gold +	en	=	golden		nearer
18.	health +	y	=	healthy		oldest
19.	old +	est	=	oldest		wanting

Now go back and write the words in each section in alphabetical order.

15

WORKSHEET 10-D

Divide the following words between the root and the suffix. Then pronounce each word as you write the root and suffix on the first two lines and the whole word on the third line.

	Root	Suffix	Word
longer	long	er	longer
fastest	fast	est	fastest
sharpen	sharp	en	sharpen
tricky	trick	y	tricky
selfish	self	ish	selfish
dressing	dress	ing	dressing
risky	risk	y	risky
greatest	great	est	greatest
singing	sing	ing	singing
frighten	fright	en	frighten
younger	young	er	younger

Unscramble the words below and spell them correctly in the blanks. They all contain suffixes. The meaning and first letters are your clues to arranging the letters in the correct order.

1. hislofo	foolish	like a fool
2. dangdi	adding	putting numbers together
3. yhtlaew	wealthy	having much money
4. galwikn	walking	slower than running
5. odenow	wooden	made of wood
6. tealcens	cleanest	the most clean

Review: A consonant suffix begins with a _consonant_ .

A vowel suffix begins with a _vowel_ .

16

Review the Doubling Rule: If a root has __one__ syllable, ends in one __consonant__, and has __one__ vowel sound, double the final __consonant__ before adding a __vowel__ suffix (hop + ing = hopping).

Add suffixes to the roots. Remember to apply the Doubling Rule when it is needed.

drum + er	_drummer_	clip + er	_clipper_
*farm + ing	_farming_	big + est	_biggest_
sun + y	_sunny_	quit + ing	_quitting_
rot + en	_rotten_	**snow + y	_snowy_
**rain + ing	_raining_	rob + er	_robber_
*help + er	_helper_	bright + en	_brighten_
fun + y	_funny_	mad + er	_madder_
**wool + en	_woolen_	*old + est	_oldest_
wed + ing	_wedding_	shop + ing	_shopping_
*fast + er	_faster_	got + en	_gotten_
hot + est	_hottest_	flop + y	_floppy_
*trick + y	_tricky_	*jump + ing	_jumping_

*Why don't you double the consonant in these words? _They end in two consonants_

**Why don't you double the consonant in these words? _They have two vowels_

18

The Doubling Rule: If a root has *one* syllable, ends in *one* consonant, and has *one* vowel, double the consonant before adding a vowel suffix.

hop + ing = hopping

one syllable
one vowel → double p
one consonant at the end

vowel suffix

Look at each root below and check for each condition of the Doubling Rule. If you have four checks, then double the final consonant before adding the suffix. If you have fewer than four checks, add the suffix without changing the root.

	one syllable	one vowel	ends in *one* consonant	adding a vowel suffix	Root + Suffix
1. sad + est	✓	✓	✓	✓	**saddest**
2. mud + y	✓	✓	✓	✓	_muddy_
3. fright + en	✓		✓	✓	_frighten_
4. cold + er	✓	✓		✓	_colder_
5. swim + ing	✓	✓	✓	✓	_swimming_
6. like + ness	✓	✓			_likeness_
7. rust + y	✓	✓		✓	_rusty_
8. bad + ly	✓	✓	✓		_badly_
9. bit + en	✓	✓	✓	✓	_bitten_
10. whip + ing	✓	✓	✓	✓	_whipping_
11. skill + ful	✓	✓			_skillful_
12. risk + y	✓	✓		✓	_risky_
13. cold + est	✓	✓		✓	_coldest_
14. wood + en	✓		✓	✓	_wooden_

17

The Drop-the-e Rule: When a root ends in a silent e, drop the e before adding a vowel suffix.

hope + ing = hoping
silent e / vowel suffix / drop the e

Underline the first letter of the suffix. If it is a vowel, cross out the silent e in the root. Write the new word.

smile + ing	=	_smiling_
froze + en	=	_frozen_
care + less	=	_careless_
smoke + y	=	_smoky_
sure + ly	=	_surely_
shine + ing	=	_shining_
chose + en	=	_chosen_
safe + ty	=	_safety_
large + est	=	_largest_
write + ing	=	_writing_
skate + er	=	_skater_
force + ful	=	_forceful_
broke + en	=	_broken_

Proofing Practice: Two common words are misspelled in each of the sentences below. Correct them as shown.

skating / frozen

1. We wanted to go ~~skateing~~ on the ~~frozzen~~ pond, but the park guard said that we had to wait for colder weather.
2. Nothing makes me ~~mader~~ (madder) than my dog's ~~diging~~ (digging) up my new plants.
3. My uncle is still ~~useing~~ (using) a ~~woden~~ (wooden) tennis racket.
4. Rob was the ~~yungest~~ (youngest) guest at the ~~weding~~ (wedding) party.

Review the Drop-the-e Rule: When a root ends in a _silent_ e, drop the e before adding a _vowel_ suffix (hope + ing = hoping).

Add suffixes to the roots. Remember to apply the Drop-the-e Rule.

use + ing	=	_using_		*wide + ly	=	_widely_
large + er	=	_larger_		broke + en	=	_broken_
*waste + ful	=	_wasteful_		spice + y	=	_spicy_
bite + ing	=	_biting_		*age + less	=	_ageless_
*amaze + ment	=	_amazement_		blame + ed	=	_blamed_
smoke + y	=	_smoky_		ride + ing	=	_riding_
*safe + ly	=	_safely_		ice + y	=	_icy_

*Why don't you drop the e from these words? _You are adding a consonant suffix._

Add suffixes to these roots.

care + ing	=	_caring_		place + ing	=	_placing_
care + ful	=	_careful_		place + ment	=	_placement_
care + less	=	_careless_				
love + ly	=	_lovely_		safe + ly	=	_safely_
love + ing	=	_loving_		safe + est	=	_safest_
love + er	=	_lover_		safe + ty	=	_safety_
large + er	=	_larger_		safe + er	=	_safer_
large + est	=	_largest_		use + ing	=	_using_
large + ly	=	_largely_		use + ful	=	_useful_
				use + er	=	_user_

Review: A vowel suffix _begins_ with a _vowel_.

The **Y Rule**: When a root ends in *y*, change the *y* to *i* when adding a suffix (*easy* + *est* = *easiest*; *happy* + *ness* = *happiness*).
Exceptions: Keep the *y* if a vowel comes before it (*play* + *er* = *player*; *joy* + *ful* = *joyful*).
Keep the *y* if adding the suffix -*ing* (*cry* + *ing* = *crying*; *study* + *ing* = *studying*).

Add suffixes or plural endings to the roots. Remember to apply the Y Rule. Circle any vowels that come just before *y* in the roots. Circle the -*ing* suffixes. Remember that these words will be exceptions to the Y Rule.

puppy	+	es	__puppies__	crispy + er __crispier__
funny	+	est	__funniest__	*pl(a)y + (ing) __playing__
*try	+	(ing)	__trying__	noisy + est __noisiest__
easy	+	ly	__easily__	**j(o)y + ful __joyful__
**bu(y)	+	er	__buyer__	lazy + er __lazier__
lady	+	es	__ladies__	*pr(a)y + er __prayer__
**pa(y)	+	ment	__payment__	sunny + er __sunnier__
healthy	+	est	__healthiest__	easy + er __easier__
party	+	es	__parties__	happy + ness __happiness__
pretty	+	est	__prettiest__	*study + (ing) __studying__

*Why don't you change the y to i in these words? __You are adding the suffix -ing.__

**Why don't you change the y to i in these words? __a vowel comes before the y.__

Another exception: *Shy* becomes *shyly* and *shyness*.

Review the rules:
The Doubling Rule: If a root has one s__yllable__, ends in o__ne__ consonant, and has one v__owel__, double the final consonant before adding a v__owel__ suffix (*hop* → *hopping*).
The Drop-the-*e* Rule: When a root ends in a s__ilent__ **e**, drop the **e** before a v__owel__ suffix (*hope* → *hoping*).
The Y Rule: When a root ends in a __y__, change the __y__ to __i__ when adding a suffix (*easiest*). Keep the y if a v__owel__ comes before it (*player*) or if adding __ing__ (*cry* → *crying*).

For each word below, write the root and then write the name of the spelling rule used to form the word. If no rule was applied, write *none*.

	Root	Rule
shady	shade	Drop-the-e
chosen	chose	Drop-the-e
bigger	big	Doubling
cleaner	clean	none
riding	ride	Drop-the-e
useful	use	none
wealthier	wealthy	Y
changing	change	Drop-the-e
greatest	great	none
funniest	funny	Y
tasty	taste	Drop-the-e
using	use	Drop-the-e
muddy	mud	Doubling
fallen	fall	none
playing	play	Y or none
smiling	smile	Drop-the-e
larger	large	Drop-the-e

WORKSHEET 10-L

Fill in each blank with one of these suffixes so that the sentences make sense. In the last four sentences you may need to add, drop, or change some letters.

-ing   -er   -est   -ish   -y   -en

1. Nathan is still pack*ing* _____ his trunk.

2. The old*est* _____ woman I know is very health*y* _____.

3. The stick*y* _____ taffy will take time to hard*en* _____.

4. Please hand me the wood*en* _____ spoon so I can stir the beat*en* _____ eggs.

5. My piece of cake is small*er* _____ than yours. But Norman has the small*est* _____ piece.

6. Will you help me length*en* _____ my skirt? The styles are long*er* _____ this year than they were last year.

7. It will be cloud*y* _____, rain*y* _____, and cold*er* _____ this weekend.

8. Martin is clean*ing* _____ his mess*y* _____ room.

9. Megan is play*ing* _____ by herself because she is self*ish* _____ with her toys.

10. Mr. Packer is luck*y* _____ to be so health*y* _____.

11. We are bank*ing* _____ at the near*est* _____ bank.

12. It is fool*ish* _____ to go fish*ing* _____ in this wind*y* _____ weather.

13. The roads were very ic*y* _____ because last night's rain had froz*en* _____.

14. Sally gave the baby the pretti*est* _____ little wood*en* _____ drum*mer* _____ boy I have ever seen.

15. Janet and Robert were sav*ing* _____ money for their wedd*ing* _____.

16. I often feel like quit*ting* _____ my job at the wool*en* _____ mill and going into farm*ing* _____.

24

WORKSHEET 10-K

Your teacher will dictate words that have vowel suffixes. Spell them under the correct heading. Remember to apply the spelling rules.

-ing	-y	-er
bringing	rainy	higher
writing	icy	fatter
digging	sunny	easier

-est	-en	-ish
fastest	wooden	selfish
prettiest	hidden	
biggest	broken	

Find and circle all of the words above in the puzzle below. The words can be found in a straight line across or up and down.

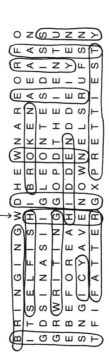

Start at the arrow and write the leftover letters in the blanks below. Work from left to right.

WHEN A ROOT ENDS IN A SILENT E, DROP THE E BEFORE ADDING A VOWEL SUFFIX.

What rule do the letters spell? The Drop - the - e Rule.

23

Read the following sentences and circle all the words from the word list that you can find.

1. Irene has (eaten) the (biggest) piece of cake.

2. The (younger) boy with the (curly) hair is (hanging) his picture (higher) on the wall.

3. Hiro is (skating) on the (frozen) pond.

4. The (sooner) you do the dishes, the (longer) you will have for (playing).

5. Ms. Harper was (planting) corn next to the (wooden) fence.

6. It gets (darker) (faster) in the months after the leaves have (fallen).

7. The children will get (dirty) (swinging) and (sliding) in the (muddy) creek.

8. The (icy) roads made (driving) (risky).

9. The (foolish) child was (swimming) in the (deepest) part of the pool.

10. It is (windy) and (rainy) today.

Take out a piece of blank paper. Your teacher will dictate three of the sentences above for you to write.

Now select ten words from List 10 and create a short story or a descriptive paragraph that uses those words. Be creative and avoid repetition!

Reading Accuracy: Demonstrate your accuracy in reading and spelling List 10 words. Your teacher will select ten words to read and ten practical spelling words for you to spell. Record your scores on the Accuracy Checklist. Work toward 90–100 percent accuracy.

Reading Proficiency: Now build up your reading fluency with List 10 words. Decide on your rate goal with your teacher. Record your progress on the Proficiency Graph.

My goal for reading List 10 is _____ words per minute with two or fewer errors.

---

long → longer → longest

Add the suffixes *-er* and *-est* to these roots. Fill in each blank with the word that makes sense in the sentence.

1. cold — People say that this winter will be _colder_ than last winter. In fact, this should be the _coldest_ winter in years.

2. fast — The ostrich is the _fastest_ running bird. It can certainly run _faster_ than a duck.

3. few — The object of the game is to make _fewer_ mistakes than the other players. The one who makes the _fewest_ mistakes wins.

4. bright — The sun is the _brightest_ object in our sky. The sun is _brighter_ than the moon.

5. strong — This coffee is _stronger_ than I like it. But the Greasy Spoon Cafe has the _strongest_ coffee I ever tried to drink.

6. sad — Ellen has the _saddest_ look on her face. She looks _sadder_ than I have ever seen her.

7. easy — My math test was _easier_ than my history test. But my English test was the _easiest_ of all.

8. large — Tomako gave Ronald the _largest_ gift. It was even _larger_ than the one he gave her.

9. hot — The sun is _hotter_ in Texas than it is in Kansas. But it is _hottest_ in New Mexico.

10. early — The _earliest_ I can come is six o'clock. If I can make it _earlier_, I will call.

11. mad — My mother can get much _madder_ than my father can. The _maddest_ I've ever seen her is when I wrecked her car.

12. pretty — I think that lilacs are the _prettiest_ spring flowers, but Justin thinks that tulips are _prettier_.

WORKSHEET 11–A

The **suffix -ed** is added to verbs (action words) to place the action in the past. For example, "Today I plant; yesterday I planted." The suffix -ed can sound like /t/ as in *jumped*, /d/ as in *called*, or /əd/ as in *acted*.

Circle and pronounce the root in the following words.

mix(ed)   yell(ed)   add(ed)   smell(ed)   kiss(ed)
water(ed)   act(ed)   brush(ed)   fold(ed)   bobsled
float(ed)   film(ed)   kiss(ed)   dump(ed)   bled
play(ed)   need(ed)   ask(ed)   end(ed)   crowd(ed)

Circle the suffix -ed in the following words. Be careful; what looks like a suffix may really be part of a root. You should have a complete word left over if you have circled a suffix.

ask(ed)   kiss(ed)   spell(ed)
hundred   bobsled   bank(ed)
fill(ed)   crowd(ed)   bled
end(ed)   stamp(ed)   land(ed)

Fill in the blanks with the root or with the root and the suffix -ed.

1. Today I wait ; yesterday I waited .
2. Today I fix the car; yesterday I fixed the car.
3. Today I call ; yesterday I called .
4. Today I help ; yesterday I helped .
5. Today it snow s; yesterday it snowed .

28

WORKSHEET 11–B

What sound does -ed have in the following words? Say the root first and then put it in the past tense. Say it aloud. Write /t/, /d/, or /əd/.

passed	/t/	acted	/əd/	planted	/əd/
camped	/t/	spilled	/d/	rained	/d/
landed	/əd/	picked	/t/	crawled	/d/
drifted	/əd/	smelled	/d/	kissed	/t/

Your teacher will dictate some words. Repeat each word, isolate the root, and spell it. Then write the whole word.

	Root		Copy	ABC Order
1.	snow	+ ed =	snowed	barked
2.	form	+ ed =	formed	dressed
3.	bark	+ ed =	barked	failed
4.	rent	+ ed =	rented	formed
5.	dress	+ ed =	dressed	pointed
6.	sound	+ ed =	sounded	rented
7.	trick	+ ed =	tricked	rolled
8.	roll	+ ed =	rolled	snowed
9.	point	+ ed =	pointed	sounded
10.	fail	+ ed =	failed	tricked

Now go back and write the words in alphabetical order.

Review: The three sounds -ed can make are /t/, /d/, and /əd/.

29

WORKSHEET 11-C

The word *jumped* is pronounced /jumpt/.
The word *played* is pronounced /playd/.

Spell the words below the way they *should* be spelled in the crossword puzzle.

/jumpt/ (1 Across)	/rockt/ (5 Across)	/seemd/ (8 Across)	/raind/ (5 Down)
/campt/ (6 Down)	/pickt/ (3 Down)	/orderd/(10 Across)	/pulld/ (3 Across)
/pressd/ (9 Across)	/milkt/ (2 Down)	/calld/ (7 Across)	/farmd/ (4 Down)

```
J U M P E D
      I     P U L L E D
  F   R O C K E D   I
  A   A   M         C A L L E D
  R   I   P R E S S E D   K
S E E M E D   E       E
  E         D
O R D E R E D
```

Your teacher will dictate some words. Isolate and spell the suffix that you hear. Then write the whole word.

	Suffix		Copy	ABC Order
1. pump +	ed	=	pumped	acted
2. sad +	ness	=	sadness	falling
3. smell +	ed	=	smelled	likely
4. act +	ed	=	acted	played
5. fall +	ing	=	falling	pumped
6. play +	ed	=	played	sadness
7. like +	ly	=	likely	smelled
8. wash +	ed	=	washed	washed

Now go back and write the words in alphabetical order.

30

WORKSHEET 11-D

If *-ed* has the /əd/ sound, it adds another syllable to the root (*add → added*). If *-ed* has the /t/ or /d/ sound, it does not add another syllable (*talk → talked, call → called*).

Read the root and then the word with an *-ed* suffix. How many syllables are in the second word?

Today I . . .	Yesterday I . . .	Number of Syllables in the Second Word
cross	crossed	1
film	filmed	1
twist	twisted	2
walk	walked	1
pack	packed	1
start	started	2
wait	waited	2
form	formed	1
roast	roasted	2
need	needed	2

Your teacher will dictate some words. Repeat the word; then say only the root. Spell the root. Then spell the suffix. Finally, spell the whole word.

	Root	Suffix	Root plus Suffix
1.	bank	ed	banked
2.	ask	ed	asked
3.	glad	ly	gladly
4.	water	ed	watered
5.	safe	ty	safety
6.	test	ed	tested
7.	shape	less	shapeless
8.	dump	ed	dumped

31

WORKSHEET 11–F

Review the rules:

The Doubling Rule: If a root has one syllable, ends in one consonant, and has one vowel, double the final consonant before adding a vowel suffix (hop → hopping).

Add the suffix -ed to these roots.

stop _stopped_	wait _waited_	beg _begged_
wrap _wrapped_	skin _skinned_	sign _signed_
ask _asked_	ship _shipped_	plan _planned_
melt _melted_	trim _trimmed_	grab _grabbed_

The Drop-the-e Rule: When a root ends in a silent e, drop the e before adding a vowel suffix (hope → hoping).

Add the suffix -ed to these roots.

use _used_	love _loved_	smile _smiled_
cause _caused_	bore _bored_	raise _raised_
dance _danced_	close _closed_	force _forced_
unite _united_	suppose _supposed_	tire _tired_

The Y Rule: When a root ends in a y, change the y to i when adding a suffix (easy → easiest). Keep the y if a vowel comes before it (play → player) or if you add ing (cry → crying).

Add the suffix -ed to these roots.

cry _cried_	carry _carried_	marry _married_
worry _worried_	try _tried_	play _played_
stay _stayed_	study _studied_	try _fried_
dry _dried_	envy _envied_	hurry _hurried_

WORKSHEET 11–E

Write these words in the correct column according to the sounds -ed makes.

fixed	yelled	lasted	chased	stepped
wanted	joined	mixed	named	skated
typed	boasted	wished	learned	rolled
tasted	signed	owned	added	bored
shopped	lifted	wrapped	needed	

-ed = /t/	-ed = /d/	-ed = /əd/
fixed	_yelled_	_wanted_
typed	_joined_	_toasted_
shopped	_signed_	_boasted_
mixed	_owned_	_lifted_
wished	_named_	_lasted_
wrapped	_learned_	_added_
chased	_rolled_	_needed_
stepped	_bored_	_skated_

Now that you have practiced the three sounds of -ed, learn this fourth, not very common, sound:

-ed sometimes says /ēd/ as in hurried, studied, envied, and some other two-syllable words that end in y in the present tense (hurry, study, and envy).

Write the past tense of these verbs and pronounce them as you write, remembering the /ēd/ sound.

bury _buried_	worry _worried_	study _studied_
marry _married_	envy _envied_	hurry _hurried_
carry _carried_		

WORKSHEET 11-G

For each word below, add the suffix -ed. Sometimes you will add only the suffix and other times you will have to apply the Doubling Rule, the Drop-the-e Rule, or the Y Rule. Check the procedure you need to follow for adding -ed. Then write the word.

	Add suffix with no changes	Doubling Rule	Drop-the-e Rule	Y rule	
1. place + ed			✓		placed
2. clap + ed		✓			clapped
3. laugh + ed	✓				laughed
4. hurry + ed				✓	hurried
5. ship + ed		✓			shipped
6. save + ed			✓		saved
7. trim + ed		✓			trimmed
8. turn + ed	✓				turned
9. happen + ed	✓				happened
10. envy + ed				✓	envied
11. suppose + ed			✓		supposed
12. bury + ed				✓	buried
13. order + ed	✓				ordered
14. spot + ed		✓			spotted
15. skate + ed			✓		skated
16. dry + ed				✓	dried
17. whip + ed		✓			whipped
18. sign + ed	✓				signed

34

WORKSHEET 11-H

Add the suffix -ed to the following words. Think first; you may need to double the final consonant, drop a silent e, or change a y to i.

snapped   studied   rented   used
typed   chased   saved   wanted
snowed   landed   shopped   robbed
tried   tired   served   barked
crawled   stepped   buried   needed

Fill in the blanks with words from above that make sense in the sentences.

1. I looked all over for an apartment that I could afford. I finally found one and rented it.

2. The dog chased the cat up into the tree.

3. Mai-Lin wanted to buy a gift for her friend. She shopped all day Saturday before she found what she wanted.

4. The turtle snapped at me as I walked past it.

5. Martha wrote her paper and Gregory typed it for her.

6. It used to upset Grandma when the dog barked.

7. The burglar robbed the bank.

8. Although it had snowed heavily, the pilot landed the plane safely.

9. Patrick put all his extra change in a bank. In a month, he had saved $15.00.

10. We served fried eggs for breakfast.

11. Alan and Carter studied for the test until 11:00 P.M. Then they were so tired that they went to bed.

12. Sam needed three stitches and a shot after he stepped on the rusty nail.

13. Fido crawled under our fence and buried his bone in the neighbor's yard.

35

WORKSHEET 11–J

Read the following sentences and circle all the List 11 words that you can find.

1. Albert (asked) if it had (rained) or (snowed) there.
2. The children (screamed) and (clapped) their hands when the seal (barked) and then (jumped) through the hoop.
3. Robert had (typed) the letter but hadn't (signed) it.
4. Emma (tried) to be brave, but she was still (scared) of the dark.
5. When the plane (landed) the (worried) woman (hurried) to catch her next flight.
6. Justin (washed) his face, (brushed) his teeth, and got (dressed) for work.
7. The band (played) as the crowd (danced) to the lively music.
8. Lucy (watered) the garden after she (planted) it.
9. Mrs. Nelson (thanked) everyone for the gift and then (called) to tell her husband.
10. After the house was (painted) Kelly (wanted) to plant roses in the flower bed.

Take out a piece of blank paper. Your teacher will dictate three of the sentences above for you to write.

Now select ten words from List 11 and create a short story or a descriptive paragraph that uses those words. Be creative and avoid repetition!

Reading Accuracy: Demonstrate your accuracy in reading and spelling List 11 words. Your teacher will select ten words to read and ten practical spelling words for you to spell. Record your scores on the Accuracy Checklist. Work toward 90–100 percent accuracy.

Reading Proficiency: Now build up your reading fluency with List 11 words. Decide on your rate goal with your teacher. Record your progress on the Proficiency Graph.

My goal for reading List 11 is _____ words per minute with two or fewer errors.

WORKSHEET 11–I

Proofing Practice: What is wrong in these sentences? Correct the spelling mistakes and re-write the sentences. The number in parentheses tells you how many mistakes are in the sentence.

1. We planed to drive to the skateing rink. (2)
   We planned to drive to the skating rink.

2. The whiped cream tasteed great on the fresh berrys. (3)
   The whipped cream tasted great on the fresh berries.

3. As I trimed the hedge, Dad mixxed up a batch of cookys. (3)
   As I trimmed the hedge, Dad mixed up a batch of cookies.

4. Judith triped on the sidewalk and droped all her shoping bags. (3)
   Judith tripped on the sidewalk and dropped all her shopping bags.

5. Peter was suppos to meet us at 5:00; we worryed when he didn't come. (2)
   Peter was supposed to meet us at 5:00; we worried when he didn't come.

6. The rober forct open the door, spoted the T.V. set, grabed it, and fled. (4)
   The robber forced open the door, spotted the T.V. set, grabbed it, and fled.

7. The children formd a circle and then dancet around the tree. (2)
   The children formed a circle and then danced around the tree.

8. When Peter stepped onto the icey sidewalk, she fell and skined her knee. (3)
   When Peter stepped onto the icy sidewalk, he fell and skinned his knee.

Mark the vowel in the first syllable long or short. Pronounce the syllables and combine them to read the whole word.

mŏp	ping	mopping	mō	ping	moping
tū	bing	tubing	tŭb	by	tubby
snĭp	per	snipper	snī	per	sniper
cŭt	ter	cutter	cū	ter	cuter
dō	ted	doted	dŏt	ted	dotted
hō	ping	hoping	hŏp	ping	hopping
spĭt	ting	spitting	spī	ting	spiting
hā	ter	hater	hăt	ter	hatter
bĭd	ding	bidding	bī	ding	biding

Pronounce the root. Then pronounce the past tense of the root. The suffix -ed does not add an extra syllable in these words because it has the sound of /t/ or /d/. Both the root and the past tense have only one syllable.

fill	filled	file	filed
robe	robed	rob	robbed
strip	stripped	stripe	striped
scare	scared	scar	scarred
tap	tapped	tape	taped

Review open and closed syllables.

1. An open syllable ends in one _vowel_, which has a _long_ sound.
2. A closed syllable has only one _vowel_ and ends in a _consonant_.

The vowel sound is _short_.

You will be able to spell troublesome word pairs such as *filed* and *filled* if you are able to tell whether the first syllable is open or closed.

Review: A closed syllable has only one vowel and ends in a consonant. The vowel sound is short (căt, ĭf).

An open syllable ends in one vowel; the vowel is usually long (lō, crā).

Categorize the following syllables according to their vowel sounds. Pronounce each syllable as you write it.

tu	dot	pla
tub	do	plan
mat	ri	hat
ma	rid	ha

Long-Vowel Sound		Short-Vowel Sound	
tu *ri*	*tu*	*tub*	*rid*
ma *scra*	*ma*	*mat*	*scrap*
ro *gri*	*ro*	*rob*	*grib*
sni *pla*	*sni*	*snip*	*plan*
do *ha*	*do*	*dot*	*hat*

Your teacher will dictate some syllables. Repeat each syllable aloud as you spell it.

1. *ta*
2. *spi*
3. *bid*
4. *mop*
5. *stri*
6. *mo*
7. *cu*
8. *slap*
9. *dot*
10. *slop*
11. *ho*
12. *scar*
13. *rat*
14. *fi*
15. *ba*

WORKSHEET 12-C

Your teacher will dictate some words. Repeat each word and identify the sound of the first vowel. If it is long, spell it in an open syllable, ending in a vowel. If the vowel is short, spell it in a closed syllable, ending in a consonant. Then write the whole word.

First Syllable			Copy	ABC Order
1. ta____	+ ping	=	*taping*	*batted*
2. rat	+ ted	=	*ratted*	*diner*
3. scra	+ per	=	*scraper*	*filing*
4. mat	+ ting	=	*matting*	*griping*
5. snip	+ ping	=	*snipping*	*matting*
6. di	+ ner	=	*diner*	*ratted*
7. gri	+ ping	=	*griping*	*scraper*
8. slop	+ py	=	*sloppy*	*sloppy*
9. bat	+ ted	=	*batted*	*snipping*
10. fi	+ ling	=	*filing*	*taping*

Your teacher will pronounce some words. If you hear a long-vowel sound in the first syllable, fill in one missing consonant. If you hear a short-vowel sound, fill in two missing consonants.

		Copy	ABC Order
1. ri p__er		*riper*	*gripping*
2. pla _nn_ ing		*planning*	*hiding*
3. gri _pp_ ing		*gripping*	*hopped*
4. slo _p_ ing		*sloping*	*pined*
5. ra _t_ ed		*rated*	*pinned*
6. sta _r_ ing		*staring*	*planning*
7. pi _nn_ ed		*pinned*	*rated*
8. hi _d_ ing		*hiding*	*riper*
9. ho _pp_ ed		*hopped*	*sloping*
10. pi _n_ ed		*pined*	*staring*

Now go back and write the words in each section in alphabetical order.

41

WORKSHEET 12-D

If a word has a double consonant after the first vowel, the vowel is short, and the root can be seen in the word. In hŏpping, hop is the root.
If a word has a single consonant after the first vowel, the vowel is long, and the root has dropped the silent e because a vowel suffix was added. In hōping, hope is the root.

Write the root in each of the following words and then pronounce the words aloud.

planned	plan	*planed	plane	spitting	spit	spiting	spite
ridding	rid	*riding	ride	*ratted	rat	*rated	rate
sniper	snipe	snipper	snip	cuter	cute	cutter	cut
tapping	tap	*taping	tape	filled	fill	filed	file
ripper	rip	*riper	ripe	mating	mate	matting	mat
sloppy	slop	sloping	slope	canning	can	*caning	cane
dotted	dot	*doted	dote	batted	bat	*bated	bate

Complete the puzzle with the starred words above.

Across
1. made level
3. more ready to eat
5. used to cut something
7. reduced force (with ___ breath)
8. recording on tape

Down
2. showed too much fondness (___ on her pet)
3. sitting on a moving animal
4. told or informed on
5. weaving with cane
6. regarded; graded

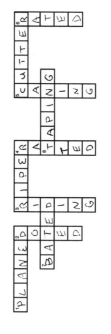

42

Circle the middle consonant or consonants in the following words. Then write the words in the correct column.

fi(l)ed   ta(pp)ed   pi(n)ed   stri(pp)ed   wi(l)ed

fi(ll)ed   ta(p)ed   pi(nn)ed   stri(p)ed   wi(ll)ed

ro(bb)ed   ri(p)er   mo(p)ed   sta(r)ing

ro(b)ed   ri(pp)er   mo(pp)ed   sta(rr)ing

Long-Vowel Words (Single Middle Consonant)	Short-Vowel or *r*-Controlled Words (Double Middle Consonant)
filed moped	filled mopped
robed striped	robbed Stripped
taped staring	tapped Starring
riper wiled	ripper willed
pined	pinned

Your teacher will dictate some words. Spell them under the correct heading.

Long-Vowel Words (Single Middle Consonant)	Short-Vowel or *r*-Controlled Words (Double Middle Consonant)
tubing cuter	tubby cutter
griped scared	gripping scarred
hoping diner	hopped dinner

Proofing Practice: Two common words are misspelled in each of the sentences below. Correct them as shown.

    planning   **dotted**
1. Janet was ~~planing~~ on wearing the new ~~doted~~ dress.

    tapping
2. My father is ~~gripping~~ about the way I am always ~~taping~~ my feet under the table.
    griping

    canned   dinner
3. Do we have to have ~~caned~~ peas for ~~diner~~ again?

    spitting
4. My baby brother is a very ~~slopy~~ eater; he is always ~~spiting~~ up his food.
    sloppy

Decide which root makes sense in each blank in the sentences below. Then add the suffix *-ing*, *-er*, or *-ed* and spell the word correctly in the blank.

1. grip   Rachel __gripped__ the dashboard as
    gripe   she __griped__ about my driving.

2. scare   Are you __scared__ that you will be __scarred__
    scar   from the accident?

3. mope   I was mad that I had to work, so I __moped__ the whole time I
    mop   __mopped__ the floors.

4. tap   Adam was __tapping__ his foot to the music as he
    tape   __taped__ it on his tape recorder.

5. pine   The girl was __pining__ away for the person in the picture that
    pin   she had __pinned__ to the wall.

6. file   I __filed__ my nails while the attendant
    fill   __filled__ my gas tank.

7. hop   Diana __hoped__ she would get a chance to see the rabbits
    hope   as they __hopped__ into the woods.

8. robe   The __robbed__ burglar was the one who
    rob   __robbed__ the bank.

9. strip   The painters __stripped__ the __striped__ wallpaper
    stripe   off the living room walls.

10. ripe   Maria __ripped__ her jacket when she reached for the apple
    rip   that looked __riper__ than the one she already had.

11. stare   The fans were all __staring__ at the teenage idol who
    star   __starred__ in the new movie.

WORKSHEET 12-G

Read the following sentences and circle all the words from the word list that you can find.

1. The (striped) cat was (staring) at the (scared) rat.
2. Roger (filed) the last of the letters before (filling) the coffee pot with water.
3. The Lennon family had (dinner) last night at the local (diner).
4. Use the rubber (scraper) to clean out the (sloppy) mess in the bowl.
5. The class listened with (bated) breath as Casper told a (scary) ghost story.
6. I (gripped) my purse as I lightly (tapped) on the door.
7. Kathy was (hoping) to get her hair cut and (styled) today.
8. The (diner) had (striped) walls and (dotted) floors.
9. This movie with the (tubby) panda has been (rated) the best of the year.
10. Chris Carson was (canning) only the (riper) peaches.
11. Henry (filed) his nails after he (mopped) the kitchen floor.

Take out a piece of blank paper. Your teacher will dictate three of the sentences above for you to write.

Now select ten words from List 12 and create a short story or a descriptive paragraph that uses those words. Be creative and avoid repetition!

Reading Accuracy: Demonstrate your accuracy in reading and spelling List 12 words. Your teacher will select ten words to read and ten practical spelling words for you to spell. Record your scores on the Accuracy Checklist. Work toward 90–100 percent accuracy.

Reading Proficiency: Now build up your reading fluency with List 12 words. Decide on your rate goal with your teacher. Record your progress on the Proficiency Graph.

My goal for reading List 12 is _____ words per minute with two or fewer errors.

WORKSHEET 13–A

A **prefix** is a word part that comes before a root and changes its meaning or forms a new word (*unpaid, prepaid, decrease, increase*).

A root is not always a complete word by itself. It may come from Latin, Greek, or Anglo-Saxon (*propel, prefer*).

Study these List 13 prefixes and their meanings.

re-	=	back, again
de-	=	down, away from
in-	=	not, in
un-	=	not
ex-	=	out
sub-	=	below, under
pre-	=	before
pro-	=	forward
per-	=	through, completely

Circle the prefixes in the following words and write them after the word.

(re)call	_re_	(un)able	_un_	(ex)tend	_ex_
(pre)pare	_pre_	(sub)way	_sub_	(per)fect	_per_
(in)direct	_in_	(in)sane	_in_	(ex)t	_ex_
(pro)gress	_pro_	(pre)fer	_pre_	(un)kind	_un_
(pro)pel	_pro_	(re)form	_re_	(sub)marine	_sub_
(per)form	_per_	(de)press	_de_	(de)bate	_de_

Now write the meaning of each prefix.

pre-	=	_before_		re-	=	_back, again_
pro-	=	_forward_		in-	=	_not, in_
per-	=	_through, completely_		un-	=	_not_
sub-	=	_below, under_		de-	=	_down, away from_
ex-	=	_out_				

Circle and pronounce the prefixes in these words. Be careful; some words do not have prefixes. You should circle twenty prefixes.

(ex)press   (un)able   dictate   (de)part

(sub)merge   pollute   (per)form   (un)fair

bonfire   (pro)spect   (pre)pare   (in)dent

(re)port   (in)flate   practice   punish

(pro)mote   (ex)cuse   dragon   (re)fuel

(de)grade   (per)sist   (sub)stance   (per)fume

(ex)cept   (sub)mit   create   (sub)tract

Match each prefix with a root to make a real word. Then say the word as you write it.

de — plain → *explain*
in — stroy → *destroy*
ex — fair → *unfair*
un — sist → *insist*

pro — vide → *provide*
pre — sist → *persist*
pro — pare → *prepare*
per — tect → *protect*

Match each prefix with a root to make a real word.

sub — crease → *increase*
pre — crease → *decrease*
in — ject → *subject*
de — dict → *predict*

ex — pect → *expect*
in — spect → *inspect*
de — spect → *respect*
re — part → *depart*

Reorder the syllables to make a recognizable word. It will be easier if you circle the prefix and underline the suffix.

(un) / <u>ly</u> / friend → *unfriendly*
vent / (in) / <u>ed</u> → *invented*
(ex) / <u>ing</u> / pect → *expecting*
ing / ceed / (pro) → *proceeding*

Match each prefix with its meaning by writing the correct prefix in each blank.

re-   de-   sub-   ex-   pre-   per-   un-   in-   pro-

1. *per* through, completely
2. *de* down, away from
3. *in* not, in
4. *re* back, again
5. *pre* before

6. *sub* below, under
7. *pro* forward
8. *un* not
9. *ex* out

The following words contain prefixes. The meaning of the prefixes will help you complete the meaning of the words.

1. unable = *not* able
2. intake = take *in*
3. refill = fill *again*
4. return = turn *back*
5. depress = press *down*
6. prepaid = paid *before*
7. exit = go *out*
8. unfair = *not* fair
9. rebuild = build *again*
10. indirect = *not* direct

11. subsoil = *below or under* the topsoil
12. preschool = *before* school
13. unborn = *not* yet born
14. incorrect = *not* correct
15. subzero = *below* zero
16. subway = travels *under* ground
17. unkind = *not* kind
18. unfriendly = *not* friendly
19. export = send *out*
20. proceed = move *forward*

Review: A *prefix* is a word part that comes before a root and changes its meaning or forms a new word.
A *suffix* is a word part that comes at the end of a root.
A *root* is the main word part to which prefixes and suffixes are attached.

WORKSHEET 13–D

Isolate, pronounce, and spell the prefix you hear in the words dictated by your teacher. Then spell the whole word, saying it as you write.

Prefix	Word	ABC Order
Sample: **Sub** ject	subject	descend
1. **pro** ceed	proceed	exclude
2. **ex** cuse	excuse	excuse
3. **pre** paid	prepaid	inhale
4. **re** spect	respect	persuade
5. **in** hale	inhale	prepaid
6. **un** able	unable	proceed
7. **Sub** stance	substance	respect
8. **de** scend	descend	subject
9. **ex** clude	exclude	substance
10. **per** suade	persuade	unable

Isolate, pronounce, and spell the root in the words dictated by your teacher. Then spell the whole word, saying it as you write.

Root	Word	ABC Order
Sample: ex **pect**	expect	decrease
11. in **take**	intake	expect
12. per **form**	perform	extend
13. sub **mit**	submit	extreme
14. pre **dict**	predict	intake
15. pro **gram**	program	perform
16. ex **treme**	extreme	perspire
17. de **crease**	decrease	predict
18. re **fresh**	refresh	program
19. ex **tend**	extend	refresh
20. per **spire**	perspire	submit

Now go back and write the words in each section in alphabetical order.

50

WORKSHEET 13–E

Fill in the blanks with the correct prefixes. You may refer to List 13. Then write the words in the puzzle.

1. to go away = **de** part (1 Down)
2. to put in = **in** sert (10 Across)
3. to get again = **re** gain (7 Across)
4. to carry out of the country = **ex** port (16 Across)
5. to move forward = **pro** gress (15 Across)
6. to go down in value = **de** crease (13 Across)
7. not fit or able = **in** ept (10 Down)
8. not helpful or nice = **un** kind (2 Down)
9. to go forward = **pro** ceed (5 Down)
10. to choose before another = **pre** fer (9 Down)
11. to refuse to stop = **per** sist (11 Down)
12. to put back = **re** turn (14 Down)
13. to disturb completely = **per** turb (17 Across)
14. act of taking in = **in** take (4 Down)
15. to call out a feeling = **in** cite (6 Down)
16. to say in front of others = **pro** claim (9 Across)
17. not fair = **un** fair (2 Across)
18. under someone's powers = **sub** ject (8 Down)
19. to blow into = **in** flate (3 Down)
20. very far out = **ex** treme (12 Across)

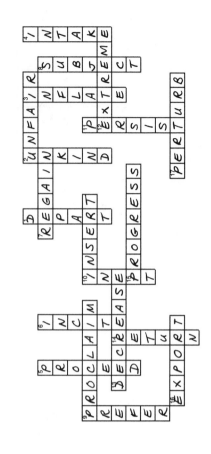

51

Students often confuse the prefixes *pre-* and *per-*. It will help you in spelling if you remember the meanings of these two prefixes:

pre- means "before"; *per-* means "through" or "completely."

Fill in the blanks with *pre-* or *per-* and write the whole word. Then copy the words under the correct heading below.

1. to tell beforehand — *pre* dict — *predict*
2. to go through or do — *per* form — *perform*
3. completely skilled; faultless — *per* fect — *perfect*
4. before birth — *pre* natal — *prenatal*
5. to put before — *pre* fix — *prefix*
6. to continue completely; refuse to stop — *per* sist — *persist*
7. to see beforehand — *pre* view — *preview*
8. to confuse completely; to puzzle — *per* plex — *perplex*
9. to pay beforehand — *pre* pay — *prepay*
10. to spread throughout — *per* vade — *pervade*
11. to keep from happening — *pre* vent — *prevent*
12. to read thoroughly — *per* use — *peruse*
13. to convince completely; to urge — *per* suade — *persuade*
14. to get ready beforehand — *pre* pare — *prepare*

pre- Words

predict	*prepay*
prenatal	*prevent*
prefix	*prepare*
preview	

per- Words

perform	*pervade*
perfect	*peruse*
persist	*persuade*
perplex	

Most two-syllable words are accented on the first syllable (*fī′ nal, stu′ dent, hop′ ping*). However, the accent pattern changes in two-syllable words that have a prefix in the first syllable and a root in the second syllable. We usually accent the root (*con fūse′, ex tend′, pre fer′*).

Draw a box around the accented root in the following words and mark the accented vowel. Cross out silent letters. Then pronounce and combine the syllables.

submit	repeat	expand	promote	unknown
inspect	propel	preside	explode	subsist
exempt	inflate	refuse	subscribe	demand
respect	express	decrease	reject	intend
perhaps	demote	exact	sublet	pervade
predict	subtract	persist	depend	inspire
excuse	proceed	prepay	perplex	insult

In a few words, the prefix is accented. Draw a box around the accented prefix in the following words and mark the accented vowel. Notice that the prefix *pro-* can be pronounced two ways: /prō/ and /prŏ/, depending on the syllabication. The first syllable of *prospect* is *pros*; thus, the vowel is short. The first syllable of *program* is *pro*; thus, the vowel is long.

prospect	product	program	income
* profit	* intake	profile	* promise
produce	subway	inboard	substance

pro- says /prō/ in:

produce
program
profile

pro- says /prŏ/ in:

promise
project
prosper

pro- says /prō/ in:

produce
program
profile

pro- says /prŏ/ in:

prospect
profit
product

* Students may divide some words into prefix and root — pro fit — or into syllables — prof it. Either answer is acceptable.

WORKSHEET 13-H

Some words can be used both as nouns (naming words) and as verbs (action words).
When the word is a noun, accent the prefix (sub ject).
When the word is a verb, accent the root (sub ject').

Draw a box around the accented syllable and mark the accented vowel. Then pronounce and combine the syllables.

Nouns	Verbs		Nouns	Verbs
recess	recess		insult	insult
record*	record		present*	present
produce	produce		permit	permit
project*	project		reject	reject
progress*	progress			

Read these sentences aloud. If the italicized word is a noun, draw a box around the prefix to show that it is accented. If it is a verb, draw a box around the root to show that it is accented.

1. The farmer had fresh *produce* for sale. — The school will *produce* a play.
2. I gave Judith a birthday *present*. — *Present* your report to the class.
3. Ms. Trabin will not *permit* smoking in her house. — You must get a driver's *permit*.
4. Martha completed her science *project*. — *Project* your voice so that we can hear you more clearly.
5. Peter *insulted* his partner. — Do not add *insult* to injury.
6. What is your best *subject* in school? — Rome *subjected* all of Greece to her rule.
7. We *progress* in learning, step by step. — Donald made good *progress* in reading.
8. Janis bought another *record* at the music store. — *Record* your progress on the Proficiency Graph.

*Syllabication differs in some words, depending on whether the word is a noun or a verb.

54

WORKSHEET 13-I

Directions:
1. Your teacher will dictate a word with a prefix.
2. Repeat the word.
3. Isolate and pronounce the prefix, saying the sounds as you spell it in the first box.
4. Isolate and pronounce the root, saying the sounds as you spell it in the second box.
5. Write the whole word on the line, saying the sounds as you spell.

	Prefix	Root	Word
1.	un	able	unable
2.	de	serve	deserve
3.	re	mind	remind
4.	per	fume	perfume
5.	ex	pect	expect
6.	in	tend	intend
7.	per	fect	perfect
8.	pre	vent	prevent
9.	pro	tect	protect
10.	ex	it	exit

Proofing Practice: Two common List 13 words are misspelled in each of the sentences below. Correct them as shown.

1. There will be a ~~reword~~ reward for the student who can ~~subtrackt~~ subtract best.
2. Please ~~exshane~~ explain why you would like to ~~exchang~~ exchange this shirt.
3. We could ~~repare~~ repair it ~~insted~~ instead of replacing it.
4. The class ~~desided~~ decided to visit the Tomb of the ~~Unnown~~ Unknown Soldier.

55

The Latin root *spect* means "to see" or "to look." Study these words, circle the roots, and underline the prefixes.

inspect   respect   expect¹

The Latin root *fect* means "to make" or "to do." Study these words, circle the roots, and underline the prefixes.

defect   perfect

The Latin root *scribe* means "to write." Study these words, circle the roots, and underline the prefixes.

inscribe   subscribe   describe   prescribe

The Latin root *tain* (from *tenere*) means "to hold" or "to keep." Study these words, circle the roots, and underline the prefixes.

detain   retain

Read the following sentences and fill in the blanks with words from above that complete the sentences. The underlined words are your clues.

1. A doctor who writes down a treatment before you follow it, __prescribes__ medical advice.

2. The police kept the suspected thief from going away. They __detain__ ed him.

3. When you look out for something, you __expect__ it to happen.

4. If you write your name underneath a statement, that means you __subscribe__, or agree, to the statement.

5. A police officer who looks into the facts of a crime __inspect__ s the evidence.

6. Work that is done completely and correctly is __perfect__.

7. A person to whom you are willing to look again for advice is a person whom you __respect__.

8. A jeweler who writes your wedding date in your wedding ring __inscribe__ s the date.

9. Sponges can absorb and __retain__ a lot of water.

*We drop the *s* in *spect* to avoid a double /s/ sound.

Many English words contain Latin roots that are not real words by themselves. When these roots are combined with a prefix, they form a real word. The meanings of the Latin roots are often a clue to the meanings of the English words.

Write the Latin roots next to the prefixes and read each word aloud.

pel = "to drive"	*spire* = "to breathe"
ex _pel_	in _spire_
re _pel_	*ex _pire_
pro _pel_	per _spire_

form = "to form"	*sist* = "to stand"
re _form_	per _sist_
de _form_	re _sist_
in _form_	in _sist_
per _form_	sub _sist_

Complete the words by adding a prefix so that each sentence makes sense.

1. You can _pro_ pel a boat by using oars.

2. The boy promised to _re_ form if given a second chance.

3. Most people _per_ spire easily during the hot summer months.

4. I could not _re_ sist tasting the frosting on the cake.

5. Shoes that are too tight will _de_ form the feet.

6. The speaker _in_ spired the crowd.

7. You must renew your license when your old one _ex_ pires.

8. The land was so poor that the farmers could barely _sub_ sist on it

9. The teacher _in_ sisted that the students complete their homework.

10. If students break the rules, they may be _ex_ pelled from school.

11. Please _in_ form Nathan about the party.

*Drop the *s* to avoid a double /s/ sound.

WORKSHEET 13–M

Read the following sentences and circle all the List 13 words that you can find.

1. Ms. Maxwell (intends) to (present) another (report) on the (subject) today.

2. We (expect) them to (explain) the new (program) at the (department) meeting.

3. I am (unable) to (prepare) my (income) tax (return) without your help.

4. (Perhaps) if we (persist) we can (prevent) the government's (destroying) the (records).

5. (Subtract) these two numbers from your gross (income) and then (record) your answer.

6. (Remind) me to (untie) my dirty shoes and (remove) them before I go (inside).

7. When the (unfriendly) shopper (returned) the broken tape deck, he (insulted) the salesperson.

8. The teacher would not (permit) the children to go to (recess) if their work was (unfinished).

9. You (deserve) a (reward) for (informing) us about the robbery.

10. The members can (prevent) (unkind) words if they show more (respect) for each other.

11. Let's (explore) some more places before we (decide) whether to (rebuild) the cabin here.

Take out a piece of blank paper. Your teacher will dictate three of the sentences above for you to write.

Now select ten words from List 13 and create a short story or a descriptive paragraph that uses those words. Be creative and avoid repetition!

Reading Accuracy: Demonstrate your accuracy in reading and spelling List 13 words. Your teacher will select ten words to read and ten practical spelling words for you to spell. Record your scores on the Accuracy Checklist. Work toward 90–100 percent accuracy.

Reading Proficiency: Now build up your reading fluency with List 13 words. Decide on your rate goal with your teacher. Record your progress on the Proficiency Graph.

My goal for reading List 13 is _____ words per minute with two or fewer errors.

WORKSHEET 13–L

Fill in the blanks with a word from the list below. Circle the word that gives you a clue about the prefix.

1. A motor that is (inside) a boat is called an _i n b o a r d_ motor.

2. The _s u b m a r i n e_ stayed (under) the water for a month.

3. Someone who can tell (before) it happens that it will rain can _p r e d i c t_ the weather.

4. Soil that is (under) the topsoil is called the _s u b s o i l_.

5. When you are tired (out) you are _e x h a u s t_ ed.

6. To plead or convince (completely) through reason or emotion is to _p e r s u a d e_.

7. Percy choked when he _i n h a l e_ d, or breathed (in) the thick smoke.

8. When you put something (under) water, you _s u b m e r g e_ it.

9. It is proper to _e x t e n d_, or stretch (out) your hand when you meet someone.

10. When you go (down) the stairs, you _d e s c e n d_ them.

11. I wish prices would go (down) or _d e c r e a s e_.

12. If you leave someone (out) of your plans, you _e x c l u d e_ them.

13. I don't want to say the directions (again) please do not ask me to _r e p e a t_ them.

14. Our French teacher always has us say (back) what she says. She thinks that it is helpful for us to _r e c i t e_ the lesson.

descend	exclude	persuade	predict
subsoil	exhaust	inhale	repeat
submerge	recite	decrease	submarine
~~inboard~~	extend		

WORKSHEET 14-A

A prefix is a word part that comes before a root and changes its meaning or forms a new word (*unpaid*, *prepaid*, *decrease*, *increase*).

Study these List 14 prefixes and their meanings.

a-	= on, in		trans-	= across
ad-	= to, toward		inter-	= between, among
ab-	= away from		con-	= together, with
ob-	= near, against, in the way		mis-	= bad, wrong
dis-	= opposite of, apart			

Circle the prefixes in the following words and write them after the word.

(a)lert _a_	(ab)sent _ab_	(inter)val _inter_
(ob)ject _ob_	(inter)state _inter_	(dis)gust _dis_
(a)cross _a_	(dis)cuss _dis_	(con)ference _con_
(ad)verb _ad_	(con)fuse _con_	(ad)vance _ad_
(ob)tain _ob_	(trans)form _trans_	(trans)fer _trans_
(ab)surd _ab_	(mis)take _mis_	(mis)place _mis_
(a)wake _a_	(ob)serve _ob_	(trans)late _trans_
(ad)mire _ad_	(con)spire _con_	(inter)face _inter_
(ab)sorb _ab_	(dis)cover _dis_	(dis)grace _dis_

Now write the meaning of each prefix.

dis-	= _opposite of, apart_		trans-	= _across_
ob-	= _near, against, in the way_		inter-	= _between, among_
a-	= _on, in_		mis-	= _bad, wrong_
ad-	= _to, toward_		con-	= _together, with_
ab-	= _away from_			

61

WORKSHEET 14-B

Match each prefix with its meaning by writing the correct prefix in each blank.

a-   dis-   mis-   ad-   ob-   trans-   inter-   con-   ab-

1. _trans_ across
2. _con_ together, with
3. _dis_ apart, opposite of
4. _inter_ between, among
5. _a_ on, in
6. _ad_ to, toward
7. _ab_ away from
8. _mis_ wrong, bad
9. _ob_ against, in the way, near

The following words contain prefixes. The meaning of the prefixes will help you complete the meaning of the words.

1. connect = join _together_
2. disabled = _opposite of_ able
3. misplace = put in the _wrong_ place
4. interstate = _between_ states
5. misspell = spell _wrong_
6. absent = _away from_ class
7. advance = move _toward_ a goal
8. adjoin = join _to_
9. dislike = _opposite of_ like
10. object = argue _against_
11. transmit = send _across_
12. away = _on_ the way

Find and circle the twelve words above in the puzzle below. The words can be found in a straight line across or up and down.

```
C H E P M R A D V A N C E E
D O F I M I S S P E L L X I N
I N T E R S T A T E T E R M E
S N A N P S B E T O W E E N
A E D I S L I K E A B S E N T
B C J A W A Y O R A J M O N G
L T O O B C M E A N E S A G A
E I N S E T C O N C M E A N
D S N T R A N S M I T W I T H
```

Start at the arrow and write the leftover letters in the blanks below. Work from left to right.

_THE PREFIX INTER MEANS "BETWEEN" OR "AMONG." ___ MEANS ___ "AGAINST." CON MEANS "WITH."_

62

Find and circle eighteen prefixes in the puzzle below. The prefixes can be found in a straight line across or up and down.

```
D O B D T A S
I N T E R E U
S P R O A B B
N R C O N U A
E E M I S N I
X A D P E R N
```

Match each prefix with a root to make a real word. Then say the word as you write it.

inter	cert	concert
con	sorb	absorb
ab	lert	alert
a	lock	interlock

ad	sleep	asleep
mis	fer	transfer
trans	lead	mislead
a	dress	address

dis	ject	object
ad	count	discount
trans	vance	advance
ob	plant	transplant

mis	test	contest
trans	take	mistake
con	mire	admire
ad	form	transform

Reorder the word parts to make a recognizable word. It will be easier if you circle the prefix and underline the suffix.

struct	(ob)	ing	obstructing
(dis)	ed	miss	dismissed
gree	(a)	ing	agreeing
sorb	er	(ab)	absorber
tain	(ob)	ed	obtained
ed	(dis)	tract	distracted

Isolate, pronounce, and spell the prefix you hear in the words dictated by your teacher. Then write the whole word, saying it aloud as you spell.

	Prefix	Copy	ABC Order
1.	mis place	misplace	abrupt
2.	trans fer	transfer	address
3.	inter rupt	interrupt	aware
4.	con spire	conspire	conduct
5.	ab rupt	abrupt	conspire
6.	ob serve	observe	disagree
7.	a ware	aware	interrupt
8.	dis agree	disagree	misplace
9.	ad dress	address	observe
10.	con duct	conduct	transfer

Isolate, pronounce, and spell the root in the words dictated by your teacher. Then write the whole word, saying it aloud as you spell.

	Root	Copy	ABC Order
11.	a loud	aloud	absent
12.	trans act	transact	admire
13.	con duct	conduct	adopt
14.	ab sent	absent	aloud
15.	dis own	disown	conduct
16.	ad opt	adopt	discover
17.	ob tain	obtain	disown
18.	mis spell	misspell	misspell
19.	dis cover	discover	obtain
20.	ad mire	admire	transact

Now go back and write the words in each section in alphabetical order.

Review: Two-syllable words that have a ___prefix___ in the first syllable and a root in the ___second___ syllable usually have the accent on the ___second___ syllable.

Draw a box around the accented root in the following words and mark the accented vowel. Then pronounce and combine the syllables.

con·fuse	a·board	tran·sact	con·sult
ad·ept	ad·join	con·spire	mis·lead
trans·act	dis·ease	in·ter·fere	a·sleep
a·larm	con·vince	ad·mire	dis·tract
ob·serve	in·ter·rupt	a·float	ad·here
mis·spell	ab·surd	dis·cuss	ab·sorb
in·ter·sect	con·tain	tran·scribe	dis·gust
con·nect	a·wake	mis·take	ob·sess

In a few words, the prefix is accented. Draw a box around the accented prefix in the following words and mark the accented vowel. Notice that only the first syllable of the prefix inter- is accented.

inter·est   inter·lude   dis·tant   mis·chief   ob·long

Review: The accent is usually on the ___first___ syllable of words with a prefix ___prefix___ and a suffix ___suffix___.

A ___prefix___ is a word part that comes before a root.

A ___suffix___ is a word part that comes after a root.

A ___root___ is the main word part to which prefixes or suffixes are attached.

Fill in the blanks with the correct prefixes. You may refer to List 14. Then write each word in the puzzle.

1. to stick to = __ad__here (11 Across)
2. going across = __trans__it (8 Down)
3. to lead in the wrong direction = __mis__lead (5 Down)
4. to scatter into parts = __dis__perse (3 Across)
5. to stop from doing = __ab__stain (10 Across)
6. to put together = __con__nect (7 Down)
7. to fit to = __ad__apt (13 Across)
8. to build with = __con__struct (7 Across)
9. to give wrong information = __mis__inform (9 Across)

10. to cross to a higher level = __trans__cend (12 Across)
11. to break apart = __dis__rupt (6 Down)
12. on or in the boat = __a__board (4 Down)
13. to agree with = __con__sent (2 Down)
14. to melt apart = __dis__solve (1 Down)
15. on fire = __a__fire (10 Down)
16. to thrust apart = __dis__pel (1 Across)

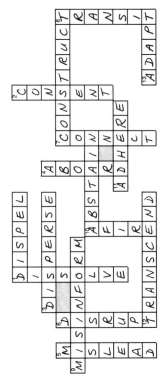

WORKSHEET 14–H

Directions:
1. Your teacher will dictate a word with a prefix.
2. Repeat the word.
3. Isolate and pronounce the prefix, saying the sounds as you spell it in the first box.
4. Isolate and pronounce the root, saying the sounds as you spell it in the second box.
5. Write the whole word on the line, saying the sounds as you spell.

#			
1.	a	head	ahead
2.	dis	cover	discover
3.	con	test	contest
4.	ab	sent	absent
5.	ob	ject	object
6.	con	clude	conclude
7.	mis	take	mistake
8.	inter	rupt	interrupt
9.	trans	port	transport
10.	ad	mire	admire

Proofing Practice: Two common List 14 words are misspelled in each of the sentences below. Correct them as shown.

1. The letter was returned because there was a ~~mistak~~ *mistake* in the ~~adress~~ *address*.
2. I hope you do not ~~objekt~~ *object* to my going ~~ahed~~ *ahead*.
3. One way to avoid ~~misspelling~~ *misspelling* words is to say them ~~aloud~~ *aloud* as you spell.
4. We can ~~controll~~ *control* the ~~diseaze~~ *disease* through drug treatments.

68

WORKSHEET 14–G

Review: If a word can function as both a noun and a verb, the noun form has the accent on the ___first___ syllable (*sub´ ject*) and the verb form has the accent on the ___second___ syllable (*sub ject´*).

Draw a box around the accented syllable and mark the accented vowel. Then pronounce and combine the syllables.

Nouns	Verbs		Nouns	Verbs
trăns plant	trans plănt		con test	con tĕst
trăns fer	trans fĕr		con tract	con trăct
trăns port	trans pŏrt		con vict	con vĭct
ăd dict	ad dĭct		con duct	con dŭct
ăd dress	ad drĕss		ŏb ject	ob jĕct
mĭs print	mis prĭnt		dĭs count	dis cŏunt

Read these sentences aloud. If the italicized word is a noun, draw a box around the root and accent it. If it is a verb, draw a box around the prefix and accent it.

1. Sign the *contract* on the bottom line.
2. Don't forget to include your return *address*.
3. The jury *convicted* him of murder.
4. What is the *object* of the game?
5. The woman *contested* the case.
6. The drug *addict* went to a clinic for treatment.
7. You will need to get a *transfer* from the bus driver.
8. Ms. Carter will *conduct* the band.

Muscles expand and *contract*.

Please *address* these envelopes.

The *convict* escaped from prison.

Many people *object* to loud music.

Who won the *contest*?

Some people are *addicted* to coffee.

Transfer $50.00 to my checking account.

The children's *conduct* was perfect.

67

Many English words contain Latin roots that are not real words by themselves. Combined with a prefix, these roots are often a clue to the meanings of the English words.

port means "to carry;" *duct* means "to lead;" *tain* means "to hold."

Use the meanings of the Latin roots listed above and your knowledge of what prefixes mean to match the words to their definitions.

		transport
		export
		deport
		reporter¹
		import¹
		conduct
		product
		induct
		deduct
		abduct
		contain
		abstain²
		retain
		detain
		obtain

1. export — to carry goods out of a country
2. import — to carry goods into a country
3. reporter — one who carries news back
4. transport — to carry across
5. deport — to carry away forcefully from a country
6. induct — to admit a person as a member
7. conduct — to lead or direct people together
8. abduct — to lead someone away by force
9. product — something led forth; the result
10. deduct — to lead or take away from
11. detain — to hold back; to keep from going
12. contain — to hold something together
13. abstain — to hold yourself away from something
14. obtain — to get; to hold something near to you
15. retain — to continue to hold in your mind

Complete the words by adding a prefix so that the sentence makes sense.

16. This milk carton **con** tains a gallon of milk.
17. My mother can **de** duct her travel expenses from her income tax.
18. This perfume is **im** ported¹ from France.
19. To be healthy, you should not **abs** tain² from exercising.
20. The United States **ex** ports wheat to other countries.

¹Note that *n* changes to *m* in this word.
²Note that an *s* is added.

The Latin root *fer* means "to carry." Write each of these words next to its definition.

confer   prefer   infer   refer   defer   transfer

1. prefer — to carry a thing ahead of other things in your mind because you like it better
2. confer — to consult (together) with people
3. transfer — to carry something from one place across to another
4. refer — to send someone for information or help
5. defer — to carry away or put off until later
6. infer — to carry your own meaning into what another person says

The Latin root *tract* means "to drag," "to draw," or "to pull." Fill in the blanks with the following words to complete the sentences. The underlined words are your clues.

subtract   extract   retract   detract
contract   distract   abstract

7. Should you be forced to draw back a statement you made, you would retract it.
8. When muscles are tightened, they are drawn together or contracted.
9. Things that pull you away from what you are doing distract you.
10. When we place a number under another number to draw out the difference between them, we are subtracting.
11. If a dentist pulls out a tooth, she extracts it.
12. An abstract idea is apart from a concrete object or a real thing.
13. An ugly frame can pull you away from the beauty of a painting; it detracts from the picture's lovely quality.

WORKSHEET 14-K

The Latin root *ject* means "to throw." Fill in the blanks with the following words to complete the sentences. The underlined words are your clues.

deject	project	object	subject
interject	reject	inject	

1. The speaker threw her voice forward until it _project_ ed to the back of the room.

2. When we throw out our arguments against someone's plan, we are _object_ ing to it.

3. A player who is downcast after losing a game often feels _deject_ ed.

4. When a nurse throws a vaccine into your arm, she is _inject_ ing it.

5. When we toss our thoughts in between other people's comments, we _interject_ our ideas.

6. The people who were thrown under the rule of a new king became his _subject_ s.

7. A writer who sends stories off to be published may have her work thrown back at her if the stories are _reject_ ed.

tend ("to stretch") and *mit* ("to send") are Latin roots in some common words. It will help your spelling if you recognize these roots within words. However, these roots don't always help you with word meanings.

Write each of these words next to its definition.

admit	submit	transmit	permit
pretend	attend	extend	intend

8. _permit_ to allow a person to do something

9. _admit_ to give someone the right to enter

10. _submit_ to yield to the power or control of another

11. _transmit_ to send over or to pass on

12. _extend_ to stretch out

13. _intend_ to plan; to have in mind as a purpose

14. _attend_ to be present at

15. _pretend_ to make believe

71

WORKSHEET 14-L

Fill in each blank with one of the words listed below.

mismatched	adjoining	convene	addict	transport
disabled	obscure	among	absorb	intersect
discovered	convict	ashore	misgivings	

1. The man was severely injured in car wreck. Since then he has been _disabled_ .

2. The socks don't match. One is dark blue and the other is dark black. They are _mismatched_ .

3. There is a traffic light where the two streets cut across each other. There is a lot of traffic where those streets _intersect_ .

4. The group will come together for a meeting. We will _convene_ before lunch.

5. A drug _addict_ is a person who depends on drugs and is very attached to them.

6. Margaret spilled water on the table. She needed something to soak it up. She found a sponge to _absorb_ the water.

7. How will I carry my belongings across town? I will have to rent a truck to _transport_ them.

8. The meaning of the poem was _obscure_ .

9. Mom likes to mingle with the crowd at a party. She has fun when she's _among_ friends.

10. You can get to Ray's room by going through Gerald's room. They have _adjoining_ rooms.

11. The judge had _misgivings_ about an early release from prison for the _convict_ .

12. The swimmers _discovered_ a beautiful piece of driftwood that had washed _ashore_ .

72

WORKSHEET 14-M

Read the following sentences and circle all the wordlist words that you can find.

1. It was hard to (translate) the letter because there were so many (misspellings) and (mistakes.)

2. Martha (discovered) that her grandfather needed a heart (transplant.)

3. We hired a mover to (transport) the goods (across) town.

4. If there is (interest,) our team can (obtain) a permit and enter the (contest)

5. Will you set (aside) your work and help me (adjust) the safety belts?

6. If no one (objects,) the teacher will (dismiss) the class (ahead) of time.

7. Albert could not (contain) his anger and lost (control) of his temper.

8. We lay (awake) (discussing) the (distant) land before we fell (asleep.)

9. It was a (mistake) to (conduct) the meeting when Jason was (absent.)

10. The children get into (mischief) and often (disagree) when they (interact.)

11. I get (confused) when you (interrupt) me.

Take out a piece of blank paper. Your teacher will dictate three of the sentences above for you to write.

Now select ten words from List 14 and create a short story or a descriptive paragraph that uses those words. Be creative and avoid repetition!

Reading Accuracy: Demonstrate your accuracy in reading and spelling List 14 words. Your teacher will select ten words to read and ten practical spelling words for you to spell. Record your scores on the Accuracy Checklist. Work toward 90–100 percent accuracy.

Reading Proficiency: Now build up your reading fluency with List 14 words. Decide on your rate goal with your teacher. Record your progress on the Proficiency Graph.

My goal for reading List 14 is _____ words per minute with two or fewer errors.

ACCURACY CHECKLIST

Megawords 2, Lists 9–14

Student _____

Record accuracy score as a fraction: $\dfrac{\text{\# correct}}{\text{\# attempted}}$

List	Examples	Check Test Scores Date:		Reading			Spelling		
		Reading	Spelling						
9. Consonant Suffixes and Plurals -ly, -ty, -ful, -fully, -ment, -less, -ness, -some, -s, -es	careless statement branches								
10. Vowel Suffixes and Spelling Rules -ing, -er, -est, -en, -ish, -y	biggest stranger planting								
11. Three Sounds of -ed /d/, /t/, /əd/	tacked mailed painted								
12. Spelling Patterns — Vowel Suffixes	diner dinner								
13. Common Prefixes re-, de-, sub-, pro-, pre-, per-, un-, in-, ex-	inside prevent								
14. Additional Common Prefixes a-, dis-, mis-, trans-, con-, inter-, ab-, ad-, ob-	abstain misplace								
Review: Lists 9–14									

PROFICIENCY GRAPH

Student_____

Goal_____

●———● Words Read Correctly

×———× Errors

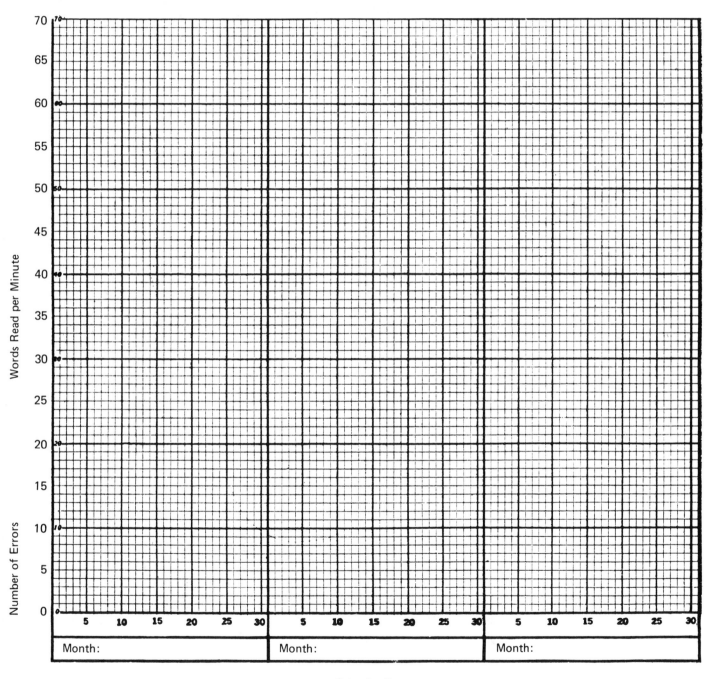

Calendar Days

EXAMINER'S RECORDING FORM — READING

Check Test: Lists 9–14

Megawords 2

Name _____   Date _____

9. Consonant Suffixes and Plurals

completely
faithfully
butterflies
government
speechless
correct _____

10. Vowel Suffixes

youngest
bringing
earlier
frighten
stylish
correct _____

11. Three Sounds of *-ed*

ordered
supposed
crowded
licked
envied
correct _____

12. Spelling Patterns— Vowel Suffixes

cuter
griping
slopped
planning
filed
correct _____

13. Common Prefixes

prescribe
unfinished
submerge
protrude
persuade
correct _____

14. Additional Common Prefixes

abduct
disabled
transcend
conspire
aboard
correct _____

Total Correct _____
Total Possible __30__

Check Test: Lists 9–14
Megawords 2

9. completely
   faithfully
   butterflies
   government
   speechless

10. youngest
    bringing
    earlier
    frighten
    stylish

11. ordered
    supposed
    crowded
    licked
    envied

12. cuter
    griping
    slopped
    planning
    filed

13. prescribe
    unfinished
    submerge
    protrude
    persuade

14. abduct
    disabled
    transcend
    conspire
    aboard